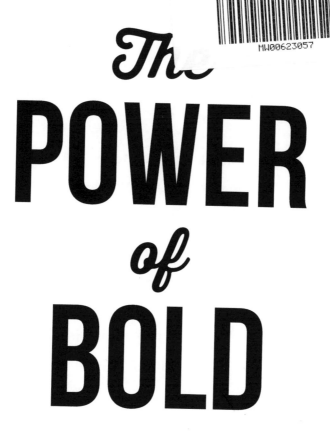

The POWER *of* BOLD

Powerful People Making Power Moves in Everyday Life

INSPIRATION BY A COLLECTIVE OF LEGACY ENTHUSIASTS

Compiled by Larthenia Howard, EdD

Publishing by Pipe Publishing

Fort Pierce, FL

ISBN 978-0-692-05980-7

Library of Congress Cataloging-in-Publication data is available.

Leadership/Business/Leadership   Motivation/Business Management

Printed in the United States

First Edition

2/17/22

To My
Ragtime friend
Tasha

It is always a pleasure to spend
time with you. Our childhood
memories and shenanigans will
forever be unforgettable!
Stay bubbly and beautiful.

All my best
Always

Shawn

CONTENTS

The Power of **Bold**

FOREWORD

New Possibilities

"Hope breeds possibilities—possibilities breed opportunities."
Dr. Howard, American author and book coach

Life has a way of sending us packages we would rather not open or stamp the delivery with, "Return to sender, address unknown". At some point, contents (circumstances) in the packages may cause hardship, loss, heartache and pain, disappointment, and even despair. These packages are unavoidable in a sense because as life goes on, so does events around us. However, if open to possibilities, new opportunities can be life giving.

Several years ago, I was volunteered by my cousin to escort her daughter, my then seven-year-old goddaughter, and several of her friends for a playdate. If you have been in the presence of young, invincible, and hormone sprouting preteen girls, then you know I was in for a lot of chattering and possibilities. After much debate and changes in the agenda, it was decided we would follow our original plans and see a movie. When we arrived, the movie I wanted the girls to see had started so we hurriedly searched for something else exciting. *Valiant*, a Vanguard production none of us had seen advertised was starting in 20 minutes. The spring chickens ("the girls") were not thrilled with the idea of watching pigeons pretend to be war heroes, however, content just to be among the wild and free, they finally agreed and *Valiant* it was. Initially, neither the girls nor I were intrigued with the film. After all, talking pigeons dressed in military armor and fighting a war is not considered a "girly" thing by most seven-year-old divas. But, minutes into the flick, the pigeons and their opposition, the Falcons, exchanged several humorous lines and our imaginations were peeked. I, particularly, began to listen more carefully to the lines of the birds and lessons of life were revealed.

Valiant, the lead character, is an extremely short bird with tiny wings. He appears to be a rather timid and an uneventful creature at first glance. Valiant lives with his mother and is viewed by the other pigeons as an all-around good guy who would always remain as a homebody. When warrior pigeons—the General Pigeon and his friends, visited a pub where many of the homeboys sort of hung out, Valiant was taken by their command for attention. At that moment, he decided that he wanted to join the cause of the fight and become a member of the General's squad in the Air Force during World War II. In his grandeur and haughtiness, the General informs Valiant, "You are not war material and besides, you would not last a week among the top birds". Valiant in his innocence replies, "I will die trying. It's not the size of your wing, but the size of your spirit"!

Les Brown, motivational speaker, has a favorite saying, "When you fall, as long as you land on your face and look up, you can get up." This is exactly what Valiant does and his actions are worth taking note. Toward the end of *Valiant*, that undersized and presumably timid pigeon who is introduced in the beginning of the movie is in the fight of his life. Several of his country's fighter jets had been shot down. Valiant found himself in the center of battle, head-to-head with several monstrous sized opposing falcons. Approaching Valiant's jet head on, the Chief General Falcon shouts, "You are no match for me, you pip squeak." To which Valiant responds without hesitation and with much conviction, "My name is Valiant"! Though Valiant was out man-powered by oversized falcons, he was not out *mind-powered*. Valiant went on to rescue several comrades from a crashed fighter jet and maneuvered through opposing fighter planes riveting heavy artillery towards him. He completed a mission to deliver a secret message from one General Pigeon to another in Germany. This message contained critical information to aid in a successful combat. His country wins the war and Valiant, and his band of small pigeon friends receive medals of honor for their heroic actions.

The term *Disrupters* has recently been used to describe big companies who have the potential and resources to the change the game of business in their niche. I propose that like these big conglomerates and Valiant too, the authors in *The Power of Bold* can be likened to this description. Each of them received contents, or life circumstances they would rather have returned to sender, but instead, made a bold decision. They changed how they played the game of life in significant and meaningful ways based on obstacles, trials, and seemingly defeat. They are gamechangers because they did what had to be done to impact the trajectory of their lives and the lives of those in their lineage. They are, by all accounts, legacy enthusiasts!

Boldness, however, is not an easy feat. It comes with a price. The price is risk that is often too difficult for most to conjure up the umph to pay. Because bold acts require some level of disruption, they are often messy and avoided. They are not the *Easy Baker Oven* recipe kind of decisions. Bold acts generally disrupt the ebb and flow of life by going against the tide. As someone frequently reminded me when I had to make difficult decisions as a secondary school principal, "Sometimes you have to tear up some stuff before you can fix it." It is true. Bold acts sometimes demand dismantling or breaking. But, in the breaking there is opportunity to build back better.

Bold requires you to believe you have whatever it takes to accomplish what you want. Too, it demands you to drown out the noise of negativity. Sometimes this negativity comes in the form of self-talk and at other times it is in the form of other people, low self-esteem, lack of confidence, or other factors. It is easy to lose sight of your heart's desires or begin to believe that you are not capable or deserving of attaining lofty goals. During these times, you must drown out the noise and tap into your inner core of beliefs of what defines you.

Remember too, it is not always necessary to know the rules of the game before stepping on the field. My son, ten-years-young at the time, reminded me of this bold move. He is an advent chess player. As an only child not having a playmate to grow up with, his dad and I often had to fill that role. Sometimes he would beg and plead with me to play chess with him but I did not know the rules of the game so I would divert his attention to something I was more familiar with. When he got old enough to recognize my tactics, he finally said to me, "You don't need to know the rules, just play and I'll teach you." Since he was convincing, I would engage him and of course he would hand me a beat down repeatedly.

On this one occasion, several days after my son swindled me to indulge in a chess slaughter, I received a phone call from the district school board office. I was instructed to report to a middle/high school to interview for a dean's position. My first response was, "But I didn't apply for a dean's job". The person on the other end of the phone assured me to just show up for the interview. As I hung up the telephone, I remember saying out loud, "I don't know anything about a dean's job. I have never done that before." Surprisingly, the next thought that came to mind was what my son had said to me just a few days prior, "You don't need to know the rules of the game, just play".

At that moment, the words from the mouth of a babe filled me with the confidence I needed. I realized then as I know now, you don't always need to know all the rules in the game of life—but you do need to get moving and play if you want to leverage possibilities around you. I went to that interview, got the job and many more doors of opportunity opened because I took the field and started to play. Life for me has certainly offered an ocean of possibilities. One of my favorite sayings is *"How you see what you see— determines what you see."* Bold acts are really a decision.

So, what is it that you should be starting, whether you know the rules or not? What have you avoided because of the fear of not knowing? What is it that you think you need to play the game, whether you know the rules or not? Winning, in most situations is not hinged on knowing the rules, but rather, acting. Some people spend so much time and effort in the planning stage that their energy fizzles when the time comes to act. Perhaps it is time to get moving! Get off the sidelines! Get in the game!

To jumpstart the journey, ponder these primary moves of **Bold**.

1. **Release your fears**. Fear has a way of immobilizing or paralyzing a person. In most horror shows, characters who are moved by fear often freeze and/or panic. The actors appear to become incapable of making rational decisions and incapacitated to take deliberate action. In real life fear can have the same affect. Instead of allowing this emotion (and that is what it is, an emotion) to stabilize you in mediocrity, use the energy to fuel your fire of ambition. Put your emotions in check. There are times when you must shake yourself. Life does not offer you a Geneva Convention agreement. Get up and get out for the battle.

2. **Unleash self-doubt**. The negatives you tell yourself about yourself can be just as damaging, if not even more, as the negatives others feed you. Affirm who you would like to become, rather than who or where you are presently. No one else can do this for you. No matter the size of your dream, the reality is that until you program your thinking to drown out the negatives, the impossible, and the excuses you tell yourself, your authentic journey will be paralyzed. Thoughts have a way of controlling actions. What you dwell on becomes your reality. But here is the delicious part—you can choose.

3. **Navigate your vision**. Navigate is defined as *"To plan, record, and control the course or position"*. You must be in control of your emotions, your thinking, your beliefs, your behaviors, and your actions to complete the vision. Likewise, your plan must be recorded in a way that clearly outline every action you will need to take, resources that will be needed, and a time frame to ensure steady progress. Create a personal mission and vision statement. As human beings we are sometimes unconsciously unaware of our thoughts, beliefs, or behaviors. Bold requires you

to be present and clear about what you want as outcomes. However, the process works only if you become a part of the process.

This may sound strange, but you have two realities:

1. The one you are currently living.

2. The unlived life within you—your yet to be manifested plans, dreams, and untapped opportunity.

But between these two realities stands a self-sabotaging part of you that works to prevent you from reaching your fullest potential. This is why so many would be writers do not write, so many aspiring painters do not paint, and why wannabe entrepreneurs never pursue their business endeavors. As compelling as your desires can be, self-sabotage uses a force just as potent to keep you right where you are and prevent you from moving toward your dreams.

In the end, many people do not do the things their hearts—inner talents—call them to do because they do not realize they are in a battle with an enemy living inside. So, what can you do to fight the good fight and win this all-important war? Act bold. Here, the term *act* is literal. When I say act bold, I mean—to imagine. Imagine yourself acting even when you are the most afraid. Assess the danger, then move. Nelson Mandela, Former President of South Africa, said it best, "I learned that courage was not the absence of fear, but the triumph over it. The brave man is not he who does not feel afraid, but he who conquers that fear." For President Mandela and countless brave ancestors, this is freedom.

Authors in *The Power of Bold* are on a mission to inspire people from all walks of life to experience freedom in confronting fear and the confidence in betting on themselves. This is a compilation of personal stories highlighting the will to overcome setbacks, setups, and upsets. It is written to help readers who struggle to confront difficult decisions, those who become immobilized by the fear of change, *and* people who are challenged by obstacles in everyday choices.

Included in this anthology are several QR codes. Hover your smartphone's camera over the code, and a video with additional material will appear. You will also find an appendix with interactive exercises toward the back of the book. We invite you to take a moment and meditate on each topic. They are designed to prompt your thinking about how you show you up in the world. Last, each author has inserted *Power Moves* at the end of their chapter. Power Moves are brief statements—takeaways, of bold thinking. Our hope is that you consider your own power moves as you walk in boldness.

Inspire your legacy,

Larthenia Howard, EdD
www.LartheniaHoward.com
www.AnchorofHopeTherapy.com
www.FromABookToABusiness.com

Malik Parker

Malik Parker is from Washington, DC. He is currently studying Integral Medicine at Quantum University. Malik is a certified peer specialist, and a writer who inspires ignite the imagination others as he delves into real life experiences that creates a storyline to draws readers into a reality as if it were their own. He is a researcher at heart and uses every opportunity to get closer to the truth, whether through speaking or writing about it.

INTRODUCTION

Understanding the Science of Bold

Malik Parker
Certified Peer Specialist

Bold – *showing the ability to take risks; confident and courageous; having a strong, vivid appearance*

Conflict – *a fight, battle, or struggle, especially a prolonged struggle; strife. controversy; quarrel*

The science of *bold* is exciting because it seeks to explain what causes some people to act even though they are fully aware of likely consequences, or the danger involved. This idea is fascinating because it is counterintuitive to how the human brain works, as one of its primary roles is to protect a person from danger. However, understanding the science of bold, this makes a great deal of sense. How? Because *bold commands conflict*. At the core of bold is duality. Before a person makes a bold move, it is common, automatic even, to question potential outcomes as too risky. For most, this is where internal red flags are triggered so they turn back.

Lived experiences, or rather the interpretation of those experiences, are fundamental in directing how you respond to conflict, circumstances, and interactions you encounter. When dealing with a dilemma you are rarely conscious of why you respond the way you do—you pull from unconscious self-imposed rules based on lived experiences. It is important to understand how you react and make decisions based on unconscious rules. To replace conflict with confidence and increase boldness, awareness of the unconscious rules governing your actions is pivotal.

How conflict functions in the brain

The human brain is made up of two large hemispheres and each hemisphere is divided into four lobes. The frontal lobe, located at the front of the brain, is responsible for thinking, reasoning, decision making, and planning. This allows you to process and manage your emotions to determine the best logical response. Emotions assign meaning and attach associations to emotional memories in the limbic system. When you sense danger of any sort, the amygdala activates a fight, flight, or freeze response. The sense of danger is channeled through the limbic system, recalling lived experiences that inform how you respond. In short, you face an inner conflict whenever a difficult situation is confronted.

The key to confident and bold responses is to unlock the unconscious mind through self-knowledge. It is critical for you to be able to access the frontal lobe (rationale thinking) as quickly as the amygdala activates, so present responses are not based solely on lived experiences. This is how you better manage instinctual inclinations to fight, flee, or freeze. Emotional wellness and strength begin with *inner-standing* your emotional nature (often unconscious) and practicing self-management to control the emotions at hand.

Brain circuits play a dominant role in conflict; you have an instinctual arousal of negative emotions. As a result, as mentioned earlier, learned experiences shape your responses based on past information. Again, this causes conflict between fear and courage. In this battle, you have a critical decision to make. You can negotiate fear (false evidence appearing real), or you can pause to trace your thoughts and decide if they are based on present realities. By no means is this an easy feat. It takes hard work and courage to override patterns the brain naturally grasps to protect you from danger. However, **Bold** is strategic. Ask yourself if you are being mindful or if your mind is full of old beliefs that do not serve you well in the present moment.

> *Watch your thoughts, they become your words,*
> *Watch your Words, they become your actions.*
> *Watch your actions, they become your habits,*
> *Watch your habits, they become your character.*
> *Watch your character, it controls your destiny.*

Lao Tzu, Chinese philosopher

There is an opportunity for growth in every conflictual confrontation. Freedom can be found in the process. You can conform to the standard or raise the bar of your expectations. Though past experiences can be a useful reference, know that their purpose is to help you navigate the present. Your power is in the present. Understanding the power you possess in the present and potential problems you face also provides great promise. The present (conscious) is a gift! There is no need to ponder in the past or funnel through the future because both only exist within the present.

How to experience conflict with confidence and clarity

Avoiding conflict is a conflict. To release *The Power of Bold*, use conflict as a channel for growth. When faced with conflict avoid the association of your feelings with a certain time in your life.

Rather, think about lessons learned. Lessons are more important than circumstances.

Here are three actions you can take to help better manage conflict when faced with Bold decisions:

1. **Meditate**. When a conversation takes place in your head have you ever wondered who is speaking and who is listening? That is your higher self (the observer) and your lower self (ego). It is the responsibility of your higher self to guide the ego in the right direction. However, your lower self has mastered the art of language and the higher self rarely speaks. Your higher self is Source. Source speaks through the sound of silence. Through meditation you begin to transcend to self.

2. **Fast**. Fasting teaches you not to submit to the demands of the body, but that the body must submit to the Source. It reveals who you are by controlling everything you are not; you are not your ego or your body. Fasting heals but most importantly it helps to connect awareness to divine nature—Source. You are infinite energy, and your inner power can be unlocked at will.

3. **Let Go**. Release the fear, resistance, and doubt that clouds your manifestation. Maintain in the present moment and be content with the past because the past is—well, the past. You are separate from your past through divine division to multiply manifestation.

The science of bold commands conflict. And, how you think about conflict will determine how you behave. If you think about conflicting decisions as a problem, you will experience problems in your decision-making. However, if you believe conflict is a portal for bold acts, you will take more opportunities to *act* Bold. I emphasize "act" because Bold is a decision. Foundational to bold are the unconscious and conscious minds.

The Six Cs of Bold Power Moves

This is what I know for sure. The act of bold is a decision made by a process of thinking. The science of bold is understood best in the context of how you think, and particularly how you think about the conflict stirred within when confronted with a scary decision. Again, knowing how the brain works to protect you will give you insight in how to better manage emotions that keep you from acting in the face of fear. You do not have to settle for less than what you want or believe you deserve. You can have the healthy relationships you want. You can accomplish the financial goals you set for yourself and your family. And most of all, you can live your best life—however you define this for yourself.

Before I go, here are six thoughts I consider when I have a scary decision. Think about how you can apply each of these the next time you would rather avoid a situation or feel compelled to back off a decision because of fear.

Communicate – Have a dialogue with yourself. Most conflict is caused by miscommunication. Sometimes this communication is with others, but often it is within oneself.

Comprehend – It is important to understand both sides of conflict to grasp a logical response. When you are in a conflictual thought, think about your thinking. What are you thinking about the thoughts flooding your mind?

Control – Control your emotions by controlling your thoughts. Do not move with every emotion you feel. Build momentum by remembering your successes. Both failure and success leave clues.

Compromise – You can settle a dispute in your brain in a mutual concession. Allow your brain to accept that it is doing its job to protect you. This conversation with yourself calms the reactive responses.

Consequence – When faced with conflict of a bold act, weigh the consequences of the potential outcomes. Determine the impact of the present moment on your future. Remember, every problem is not worthy of your attention.

Closure – Tie a bow. This simply means to decide. Harnessing the power of bold involves deciding when to pull forward and when to pull back.

The ancient Emerald Tablets of Thoth states "As within, so without. As above so below". The thoughts you hold in your mind have an incessant ripple effect in your life and the lives around you. Conflict you face on the outside reflects emotional conflict on the inside. Your brain is constantly rewiring itself to suit information you feed it. If you think in terms of confidence, you will begin to see a reflection that reshapes your reality. Mindset matters.

> "If you haven't confidence in yourself,
> you are twice defeated in the race of life.
> With confidence, you have won even before you have started"
> - Marcus Garvey, Jamaican activist

Power Moves

- Know thyself; understand how you process the meaning of circumstances and events in your life.

- Question your thoughts for truth and validity. Are you operating in fear?

- Meditate to reveal unconscious memories associated with faulty thinking and those that no longer serve you well.

CHAPTER 2

India Gary-Martin

India Gary-Martin is a 25-year veteran of financial services and member of the Forbes Coaches Council. A career expat, she spent 20 years of her career in Europe and Asia holding global COO, CIO, and CTO roles. In her final role at JPMorgan, she was managing director and Global COO for Investment Banking Technology and Operations, where she had multi-billion-dollar budgetary management for a staff of more than 15,000 people in 40 countries.

India is now an entrepreneur and sought-after leadership expert and strategist who works with corporate boards, CEOs, and their leadership teams from around the world. A diversity, equity, and inclusion practitioner, with a focus on race and gender equity, she has taken more than 6000 people through her racial equity capacity building workshops since the death of George Floyd. She is on the coaching faculty of Georgetown University's Executive Master's in Leadership Program and the faculty of Corporate Education at Howard University for the Diversity, Equity, and Inclusion Certificate program. During her time in Europe India was named one of the top 50 businesswomen in Europe and to the UK Power List for successive years. India speaks fluent French and functional Japanese. She sits on the board of Euromoney Institutional Investors PLC, is married with 3 children and lives between Washington DC and London.

Risk It

Taking Risks When the Stakes are High Risk

India Gary-Martin
Leadership for Exes, Founder & CEO

> *If you do not have courage,*
> *you may not have the opportunity to use any of*
> *your other virtues.*
>
> **Samuel L. Jackson, American actor**

"This is the right thing to do." As I had the conversation with my husband about selling our house to fund my business that was in distress, I thought it was the right thing to do. In hindsight, I still believe it was the right decision. If my company went under, my team and their families would suffer which was unconscionable for me. The stakes were high, and I was taking a huge risk. We have three children and the decision we had to make was about putting our own livelihood at risk versus the exponential risk of the company going under to my team and their families. It was agonizing. I did not know if the injection of cash would save the company (this was the risk), but I knew it would buy time. That meant I could survive, and my team could too, at least for the near term (the reward).

When I think about taking high stakes risks, my first thoughts are people fleeing war torn countries for better lives or enslaved people in the US who risked their lives to escape the shackles of slavery—the kinds of decisions that are the difference between life and death. These examples might sound extreme but when you think about what everyday people have risked in the most extreme circumstances, it quickly provides perspective on the kinds of risks that we might take from places of relative safety. The thing about high stakes risks is that they are relative to *your* risk appetite and how much you need or want the outcome. While safety is also relative, most of the risks you take are not risking your life or livelihood. What may be high stakes risks for some may not be high stakes for others. The refugee fleeing a war-torn country would likely think what I consider to be a high-stake risk, a luxury.

> *"If you don't risk something, you'll risk even more."*
>
> **Erica Jong, American novelist**

High stake risks are scary but worth it

Playing it safe is okay. There is nothing wrong with wanting stability and safety but there is no reward without risk and if you do not risk *something*, you risk even more. You miss the opportunity to walk in your power. You could miss something that will transform your life or the lives of others. Transformational opportunity rarely comes without risk and is often high stakes. High stakes are scary. As opposed to thinking about the opportunity, many of us worry about what we could lose—preventing us from taking any risks at all. Comfort and safety are essential human needs. While lots of people do not have it—those that have it want to keep it and those that do not have it are always seeking it.

What prevents you from taking risks? How might you walk through your fears to take risks when the stakes are high? Fear is the number one thing that stops people from taking risks, particularly when the stakes are high. To position yourself to be able to take risk, practice by taking risks when the stakes are low. If you wanted to climb Mount Everest, that is not where you would start. You would likely take some time training on smaller mountains. The ability to take risk is exercising a muscle, just like any other skill that you learn. Here are six ways you can practice taking risks:

1. Identify a small risk and take it. Notice how you felt when you took the risk and how you felt when it paid off.

2. Understand that risk is akin to uncertainty. You will not know for sure what the outcome will be. Practice being okay with not knowing.

3. The discomfort you will experience is normal. Comfort while taking risks isn't taking a risk.

4. You can mitigate challenges with good planning and preparation.

5. The bigger the risk, the more planning and preparation you need to do.

6. Plan for the challenges that will inevitably occur as opposed to hoping for the best.

You may to pivot in the process

It is not uncommon to have to pivot to get to an outcome or mitigate a risk. How much easier do you think it would be if you were prepared and had sound options available when you needed to pivot as opposed to having to pivot on the fly? I have done both and the pivoting without a plan did not end well.

Keep change in perspective. Pivoting is nothing more than changing course to get the outcome you want in a different way than you would have originally planned. One of the biggest keys to taking risk is not being so fixated on the *how* that you miss other ways to get to the *what*. "If you face an obstacle, you don't have to face it head on, you can always go around it." My basketball coach from high school used to always say this. She would stand firmly in the way of the basket and taught us to go around her. I still made the basket, but instead of making it from down the lane in the center, I made it from the left or from the right. There are more ways than one to skin a cat. It is easy to get stuck when things do not go to plan and for those who are more plan oriented, the thought of changing course can be daunting. So, instead of making the pivot this thing that is outside of your plan, make it a part of your plan. If planning is your thing—plan for what you will do when the various scenarios arise. You cannot plan for everything but doing as much as you can make things a bit easier. Some find pivoting easier and planning hard. There is no right or wrong answer. The only answer for you is the one that is aligned to *your* risk tolerance and the journey that you choose to get to your outcome.

I have often toiled with the question around whether a pivot is tempting fate—if it did not work out, maybe that is how it is supposed to be. Maybe so but there is a balance to strike between going against your gut and trusting your gut. Trust your gut. The cliché little voice is really a thing and if you listen to it, you will know when you have reached the end of the road. That being said, there is *always* another option. Making the decision to pursue it takes you back into the cycle of weighing your tolerance for that risk. Eventually, you get to a point where the risk is clearly too high. Do not stop until you get there. For example, I love watching high stakes card games...especially poker. Watching players thrown in their cards when they know they have reached their risk threshold is thrilling. There is always a victor. Whether by skill or by chance, they believe that the inevitable reward is greater than the risk. Ultimately, we all have choices. You can choose to go left or choose to go right. If you make the wrong turn, you can make a U-turn and start again. You may start again with less than you began with the first time but sometimes the beginning is a good place to start. The end is relative as is the time it takes to get there.

> *"When I dare to be powerful, to use my strength in service of my vision then it becomes less and less important whether I am afraid."*
>
> **Audre Lorde, American writer**

When you are taking a risk that only impacts you, even if the stakes are high, the stakes are lower than if the risk you are taking impacts other people. The risk to others often stops me in my tracks. High stakes risk compounded by worry for others can really send those fears into overdrive. What if I am not successful? What will people think of me if it doesn't work out? Are they going to lose out because of my risk? Some types of risk require more courage than others but if you are making them in service to your vision, fear becomes a lesser factor in moving forward. Stop and ask yourself these questions:

1. Is the risk that I am taking in service to my vision?

2. Is the risk aligned to my personal cause, or even the greater good?

3. What will I gain from taking this risk?

4. Is the *possibility* of what I will gain greater than the fear of not doing it?

I am awed by the courage of people who put their lives on the line in service to others. Firefighters go headlong into burning buildings, civil rights activists' risk social and physical persecution, soldiers go into crossfire to protect liberty, a passerby pulls a person from a car moments before the car explodes—where do they get the courage? What makes these ordinary people do the extraordinary? Why do they take these risks? They find strength in their vision. Even when things get hard. While the risks they take may also be in aid of themselves, their compunction to protect others is greater than their fear of not taking the risk.

Think about Harriet Tubman. She put her life on the line 19 times to bring more than 300 slaves to freedom without ever losing a single person. Her belief that enslaved people should be free was greater than her fear for her own life. If she were caught, she would have surely been killed. I am not suggesting that we will all take risks as great as the risk she took but we all have the capability if we align our goals to our motivations in a purposeful and intentional way.

Risk is about choice

The journey to save my business was not life or death in the physical sense but losing the company without giving my team the time to find alternative employment could have caused significant economic hardship to them and their families. While our main business was manufacturing products, I would not have been as successful without a committed team who always pushed through in challenging times. Since I was operating from a place of strength in service to my vision, I understood that the risk that I was taking was not about selling my house, it was about the fear of displacing my family from our home and what it would mean for us. The risk was also about how and when I would be able to own property again given rising property costs and that sinking the money into my company would mean that I would not necessarily have the cash at hand to start over again in the near term. Ultimately, the decision I made was to save the livelihoods of other families at the risk of discomfort to my own.

For some people this would be a non-starter. Risk your family's comfort for others? No way! Lots of people asked me when I was going to fold the business as it began to decline. The thought that I might actually sell my house to fund something that was clearly not going to work seemed silly to some. But to me, it really was about my team. I knew deep down that it was only buying time, but it was worth the risk to stay true to my vision of creating a first-class product while being one of the best employers I could be. I have always known that I am a survivor and can make a way out of no way. While I knew selling my house was a huge risk, I have always landed on my feet, even if I landed on my butt first. High stakes can be scary but is all a part of the journey. There are no absolutes and the path you choose is as important as the destination.

Reward does not come without risk but remember:

1. Listen to your intuition and trust your gut.

2. Know that everything will be okay even if it is not what you planned.

3. Find strength in staying true to your vision.

4. Only you can determine your risk threshold.

Risking it when the stakes are high takes courage but can offer life's greatest rewards. Do not be afraid of risk. Plan for it, measure it and mitigate it. If you trust yourself, you're in good hands.

Power moves:

- Be aware that high stakes risks are relative to *your* risk appetite and how much you need or want the outcome.

- Know your risk threshold.

- Recognize that risk is a choice.

18   The Power of **Bold**

CHAPTER 3

Colonel Terri L. Bailey

Colonel Terri L. Bailey is the Command Surgeon, Air Force District of Washington (AFDW), Joint Base Andrews, Maryland. AFDW is the Air Force Component to the Joint Forces Headquarters-National Capital Region and is responsible for organizing, training and equipping combat forces for aerospace expeditionary forces, homeland operations, civil support, national special security events and ceremonial events. AFDW also provides major- command-level support for 33,000 military and civilian personnel assigned worldwide.

Colonel Bailey earned a Bachelor of Science degree in Nursing from Eastern Kentucky University and received a direct commission into the Air Force while working as a clinical nurse at Mt. Sinai Medical Center, Cleveland, Ohio. She has worked in a variety of operational, education and training, and leadership positions as an Active Duty and Reserve officer, as well as a civilian nurse. Her experiences include inpatient, outpatient, staff development, aeromedical evacuation, operating room, recovery room, emergency room, executive officer, protocol officer, chief nurse, squadron, and group commander, as well as deployments in Iraq and Afghanistan.

They Said No
Overcoming Rejection with Gusto

Terri L. Bailey
United Stated Air Force, Colonel

> *"Success is to be measured not so much by the position that one has reached in life as by the obstacles which he has overcome while trying to succeed."*
>
> **Booker T. Washington, American educator**

At some point in life, you will face rejection. How you choose to deal with that rejection (or not), can shape who you are at that time or who you become in the future.

Rejection can be subtle or obvious, unintended, or malicious. But it does not matter how it happens; the results can be damaging either way. Your reactions and responses become crucial to your development and growth. If you do not recognize or deal with rejection, there may be risks to your physical, mental, spiritual, or social well-being.

As I took this trip down memory lane, I analyzed how I responded to diverse situations that involved some form of rejection. I uncovered some suppressed memories and emotions as well as some unresolved scars. I also recognized some of the consequences (good, bad & ugly) which resulted from my actions and inactions. Rejection is a powerful influencer.

Believe it before you see it

For as long as I can remember, I wanted to become a nurse. I often heard my teachers talk to our class about going to college. It seemed to be an expectation of every student. Surprisingly, I never heard my parents talk about college. No one in my family, that I knew of, had gone to college. But when I got to high school, not only did I hear my classmates talk about college, but they were specific in terms of which college they planned to attend. It was very natural and common speak among my classmates. It was not common talk at all in my neighborhood or circle. The first time I mentioned my hope of going to college to my parents, I was high school. I got vastly different reactions from the two of them. My mother was all in, "Of course my baby is going to college" she said. I was somewhat surprised because she had never mentioned college to me before. When I mentioned it to my father, well his reaction was surprising in another way. As he was driving the car, he looked over at me in the passenger seat and laughed. I did not know what to do with that. Did he think I was telling a joke? Neither one of us said another word during the ride.

Through the support of my high school guidance counselor, I navigated the process of applying for college. I received offers from multiple colleges to run track. I really had a desire to play soccer instead, feeling really burnt out with track. I had decided I would concentrate on getting a nursing degree. I was accepted to the University of Cincinnati, along with one of my friends and neighbor. We decided to become roommates. We got our packing lists and split the purchases. Nothing could contain the excitement we felt, though not as excited and proud as our parents. It turns out, my dad was not against me going to college. Being the primary breadwinner of the family, he did not know what that looked like. He did not know how he was going to afford sending me to college. In his mind, rich people sent their kids to school. He knew we were not rich, in fact, far from it. What he did not realize was there many avenues of support for students. Naturally, he did think it was a joke that he would ever be able to afford to send me to college. However, he did warm up to the idea over my high school years. He began thinking "How can I support" verses "No way I can support." Part of his mindset change was my steadfast affirmation that I was going to college. I continued to speak it, and, in my mind, it was going to happen, one way or another.

The Friday prior to Labor Day, my dad and one of the high school assistant track coaches showed up to my summer job at the community center. It was very odd. What were they doing here? My dad asked me to come talk to them for a minute. My Coach started the discussion. "There is a college who wants you to come run for them on their team. They are willing to give you a scholarship." I immediately responded, "No, I'm going to UC. I've already been accepted, and I have a room assignment and a roommate." My dad sat quietly and listened. My coach went on and on talking about how much talent I had, and I should not waste it. He explained how this was an incredible opportunity, you have had time to rest and recover over the summer. Just as I was about to speak, my dad interrupted and said in a clam and quiet voice, "I want you to go and take the scholarship." That was it. Daddy's girl always listened to her dad. I never wanted to disappoint him. "Ok, I'll go." The coach let out a sigh of relief. As he began filling me in on the details, my dad kissed me on the forehead and left because he needed to get to work. The coach told me that the school had already started two weeks ago, and I needed to be there on Monday to get registered and start my classes on Tuesday. In just a few minutes, my whole world changed.

My dad and brother drove me to school. I rode with my dad and my brother drove my car. It was a 2.5-hour drive, but it seemed like an eternity. We arrived on the scene of a beautiful campus.

Welcome to Eastern Kentucky University, the Home of the Colonels—the bright maroon and white letters read. I did not have any time to research the university before my short-notice departure from home. I spent the time saying goodbye to friends and families and getting supplies I needed. I was no longer going to be just 20 minutes from home. I was going away. I was in another state.

The campus was sprawling with young men and women, both Black and White—more White than Black, all looking happy go lucky without a care in the world. The EKU Assistant Track and Field Coach met us and led us to my temporary dorm room. The coach provided met the keys and instructed me to be ready tomorrow morning at 8:00 in the morning and he would take me to the Registrar Office. My dad and brother unpacked my things from both cars and quickly got me settled. Dad had to go to work that night, so he needed to get back home and rest before his shift started. And just like that, I was alone. But I did not feel lonely; I was anxious and happy and excited. I was in college...a dream come true.

Moving in the pain of rejection

Track and Field was a means to an end as far as I was concerned. I had no illusions of making it to the Olympics or having a career in track. My goal was to become a nurse. I focused on my grades and worked hard to keep up with the pre-nursing class requirements so I could apply for nursing school on time. I was granted permission from the track coach to take more than the 12 credit-hour limit during track season because I maintained a good GPA. I even began tutoring some of the other pre-nursing students. All was right with the world. I was maintaining a healthy balance of school, track, and a social life.

After two years of prerequisites, it was now time to apply for Baccalaureate School of Nursing. It was Spring Break, and the track team was in Florida competing at the Gainesville Relays. I called home to check in as I always did when the team traveled to different destinations. After the customary hellos and details of where I was staying, my dad began to apologize. "I'm sorry you didn't get in" he said. 'Get in what," I responded. He went on to say he got a letter from the school, and it said I was not accepted into the nursing program.

The world stopped moving for me in that moment. All I kept thinking was, how did this happen. How could they make such a mistake? I told my dad, "They made a mistake, this is a mistake". He tried to calm me down. "Don't worry about it. You can try again." I was not having it. "No dad, this is really a mistake. I will take care of it when I get back to school." I could hear the sadness he felt for me over the phone. It was not disappointment, he felt sorry for me. He knew how much I wanted this, and he felt helpless. Soon my feeling of confusion turned to anger. How dare they make such a mistake? They got my dad thinking I did not do what I needed to do—that I was not good enough. They are going to hear from me, I thought. I could not wait to get back to school to get this mistake rectified. The news put a damper on what was supposed to be college Spring Break.

The first business day after I returned, I called the School of Nursing and requested to speak to the Dean. The person on the phone asked me who I was and why I needed to speak to the Dean. I informed her that they sent a letter to my dad stating I did not get accepted in the nursing program and they made a mistake. The lady put me on hold and when she returned, she said, "I just looked up your information and it was not a mistake." I quickly refuted her. "It was a mistake." I told her I had spoken to several pre-nursing students, many of whom I had tutored, and they all were accepted. She put me on hold again and when she returned, she said she was going to schedule an appointment to speak to the Dean. I went to the appointment the next day. The Dean and I sat in her office and the conversation went something like this:

Dean: "How can I help you?"

Me: "Someone sent a letter to my dad saying I wasn't accepted to the nursing program, and it was a mistake."

Dean: "I've looked at your record and there is a good chance you will get in next time. We have criteria we follow, and you did not get accepted this go round."

Me: "All I know is, all the students I tutor were accepted. And I know for a fact my GPA is higher than theirs. So I don't know how the mistake was made, but somebody needs to send my dad a new letter."

Dean: "If we have some additional openings, you will be considered."

Me: "It is clear to me you all made a mistake. And now my dad thinks I'm not down here taking care of business. I know at least a half dozen students who were accepted who have lower GPAs than me and they were accepted. I expect my dad to get a new letter."

I felt myself getting angrier and angrier as the meeting went on. When I get too angry, I start crying and I did not want her to see me cry. So, I got up and walked out and went back to my room. I was shaking like a leaf, thinking to myself...how dare they do this to me and my dad? I was so embarrassed; my friends all assumed I was accepted. They were shocked to learn the news. "How could you not get accepted?", many responded. I simply replied, "They made a mistake."

For years, I genuinely thought the university made a mistake. Perhaps they did and could not own up to it. Maybe it was more nefarious than that...I will never know for sure. But my naivety coupled with my relentless efforts gave them the opportunity to do the right thing. Two days after my meeting with the Dean, I received my Acceptance Letter, and my dad received the same letter a week later.

The punches kept coming

Later I discovered that getting in the nursing program was the easy part. The classes became tougher and tougher. Students dropped out like flies, some for academic reasons and others decided it was not the career they wanted. My school-track-social life balance became more challenging, especially when I started my first year of hospital clinical training. This was a new element—I got hands-on training with real patients. This was the real deal.

I will never forget my Clinical Instructor and the first feedback/evaluation session with her. As we sat in her office, she high-lighted several areas where I needed to improve. This was my first feedback/evaluation session, so I did not know what to expect. I thought it was perfectly normal for her to point out all my flaws and mistakes without providing any positive feedback. However, what shocked me to my core was when she stated and wrote on my evaluation form "You are cognitively inferior." She said it as if it was a so matter of fact. Then she went on to say, "Because you are cognitively inferior you are going to have attend clinical training twice a day. You will attend clinicals with your class during the day, and in then you will return in the evening to get some additional training and practice. Any questions? If not, sign here" Questions? I was speechless. All I could think about was, inferior to what? What if I do not sign? What if I do not go to clinicals twice? What is happening?

Somehow in the midst of my shocked state, I signed the document. I slowly walked back to my dorm room. My mind continued to race. I immediately regretted signing the document. I wavered back and forth to myself. You had to sign it, otherwise they would kick you out the program. Maybe I should go talk to the Dean. No, I was sure she did not want me back in her office. What do I do? Do what you have to Terri. You are going to get that degree no matter what!

The sweet of victory

Graduation Day was a day I will never forget. I was the only African American in my class. My family showed up and cheered for me like I was the Valedictorian. I was not.

There were times when I quit, gave up or just failed to thrive. In those moments I forgot who I was—who I belonged to, who I serve. The consequences were inevitable. Fortunately, my family of believers continually poured into me. Their unwavering love and encouragement became the foundation that helped me get up, push through, and overcome some of my most painful rejection scars.

power moves:

- Do not quit on yourself. Do your best. Victory is almost always just around the corner.

- Determine your own path, no one has the authority to define you.

- Remember who you are. Start/build your legacy.

CHAPTER 4

Jennifer Jackson

Jennifer Jackson was born in Hampton, VA to a military family. She was raised in Fort Washington, MD and is now living in Cincinnati, OH, by way of Charlotte, NC. She is a proud mother of two delightful daughters in their early twenties. She is committed towards serving her community and others and does so through active membership in service-oriented organizations. Jennifer is a graduate from Hampton University and has a long and successful career in programming and data management and analysis.

Now that we have that part out of the way, Jennifer is also a person who loves to have fun. In her earlier years, going to clubs and card games, Spades, in particular, were her passion! As she has somewhat settled down, Jennifer still loves to listen to all types of music, read, watch movies, and keep active. Staying active is a must for Jennifer. Whether it is through distance walking, recreational sports, Pilates, or weightlifting, she finds enjoyment in all that she does.

Jennifer's newest journey is one of self-improvement and self-empowerment. Now that she is an empty nester and recently divorced, being and staying physically fit and financial independent is her current priority. Jennifer also stives to set an example for her daughters, that they too can chart their own destinies.

The Empowerment Plan
Take Life by the Horns

Jennifer Jackson
Fitness Coach

> *"Never be limited by other people's limited imaginations."*
>
> **Dr. Mae Jemison, American engineer**

How did I get here?

Is this really my life? As I look at the circumstances and life events that got me here, I sometimes wonder if they have been a blessing or if I am just constantly overcoming unfortunate and inevitable barriers to happiness. One could say that age is inevitable, and this is quite true. Life in my 50's has not been what I expected at all! My fifties started on track; married for over 20 years, two wonderful daughters who were in college, employed, living in a beautiful home, friends, socially involved, healthy and active. Perfect, right? So, what happened?

Let us start with marriage. I am fortunate to have married a genuinely good and dedicated man who provided well for his family. He is a man who is well respected in his industry. I was living the good life as a wife of a top executive for years. Everything was great, at least on the surface. But as I reached my fifties, I realized that for me, there was a crucial missing element—happiness. As the years grew in our marriage, I was growing away from my husband and away from my desire to remain married. I had been holding in these feelings for the sake of my family and at the expense of my emotional wellbeing. I had to do one of the most difficult things in my life. I had to tell my husband that I wanted a divorce.

Okay, next. My employment status is something that some would find fortunate. For many years, I was blessed to be able to stay home with my children and be involved in all aspects of their development. It was only after they had gotten older and no longer needed me to be as involved, did I go back to work. It was a thrilling start as I went back to work as a consultant. It was not a full-time commitment, so I was able to set my own hours and manage my personal activities, namely, competitive tennis, along with my kids and work schedule, seamlessly. To be honest with you, it felt good to get that check in the mail. There is a level of independence I felt as I got paid.

Unfortunately, this level of freedom did not last long. It burst along with the economic bubble. As the economy went down-hill, I made the decision to accept the offer of full-time employ-ment with my client. No more tennis, no more working from home. I was now back to the 9 to 5, seated at a desk in the of-fice routine. So, what is wrong with this? Nothing, for 11 months of the year. It was during that single month that I was subjected to sit during a performance review and listen to someone review my work, which was always stellar, and then make excuses as to why my pay was continually not reflective of me and what I pro-vided to the team. This is when I felt most frustrated and pow-erless. Once I reached my fifties, this became more than just a frustrating annoyance, it was downright insulting.

Deep held emotions, work frustration and a sharp decline in physical activities, led to me finding a new source of emotional support. You guessed it, food! I already loved to have my taste buds delighted. In fact, I cannot really say that there are ma-ny foods that I do not like or would not try. I found myself less motivated to push away my plate, or to exercise restraint as to what, when or how much I "snacked". As the years went on, so did the pounds. I did not notice it at first. As I was not able to fit into my clothes, I just bought the next size up. I was not seeing the change that my body or health was going through until I reached numbers too high on the scale and size chart to continue to ignore. It was when I reached my fifties that I saw what I had done to myself and was horrified. I was lethargic compared to how I used to feel and was falling into an ever-deepening depression.

My "Why"

What is "My Why" is a catch phrase I have heard for many years. I have heard at nearly every conference or motivational Zoom meeting I have attended lately. For me, "My Why" is the key reason for what I do or will do in my life. My first step to self-empowerment was to determine my "Why's". Personal preservation, financial independence and my daughters were my foci. These were what drove me to continue this path of self-empowerment. They kept me moving forward despite the obstacles that kept trying to derail my progress.

There was no way I could continue to gain weight. It was causing sleep issues as well as a decrease in energy. I had become self-conscious and did not like to be in pictures. There is nearly five years of my life, where I am not pictured with my family, other than a face or upper body shot, because I could not stand how I looked. Crying every time I was in a dressing room had become routine.

Thank goodness I was self-aware enough to know I was on a downward spiral that would not end well. My turning point was the upcoming high school graduation of my oldest daughter. There were going to be family and friends that had not seen me in person in years. You may think it is vanity, but so what? This was the trigger that started me on a path that would lead to changes in other aspects in my life. It does not matter what is your trigger. Use whatever it takes to get you on a path to improvement.

As I started making a change in my health and physical state, I knew I needed to change other aspects of my life. I had to face my fear of addressing my marriage and being honest with my husband. Mental and emotional health are areas that are often ignored or avoided. For me to continue to improve and stive for happiness, I had to make be honest with myself. Doing this involved professional counselling to address my anxieties. It helped tremendously.

With the realization that my marriage was going to eventually come to an end, came the realization that my finances would be drastically impacted. Hey, for some, that is a price that must be paid to gain back emotional stability. This factor is so impactful, that there are many who will stay where they are rather than lose their financial safety net. In my case, I was fortunate to have others in my circle who have entrepreneurial mindsets. This is how the seed was planted in my spirit that I would be ok and would find a way to make it. I would find the right options for me to be the master of my fate.

Making so many changes was not a walk in the park. None of this was overnight. It took years of self-doubt, circumspection and then action. Ultimately, it took a leap of faith in myself. As I started this journey, I aimed to set an example to my daughters that they have the power to control their lives. They do not need to stay in any situations that are detrimental to their well-being. Options and resources are out there. Find them, use them, and seek your happiness.

Decisions, decisions, and more decisions

Whew! We got through the hard parts. It is all good from here, right? Wrong. The next phase was just a different level of anxiety. What should I do, what can I do, how can I do it? All good questions. Finding the answers took me through another phase, fear of failure, and self-doubt. The one thing I was doing well was changing my physical condition. I was working out and improving my diet. It was not easy or quick, but the results were rewarding. It began with me trying many different fitness options and staying with the one that worked best for me, weightlifting. Hiring a trainer was key to me staying on task and getting the nutritional guidance I needed to drop 8 dress sizes. Yes, from a 16 to a size 8. Not overnight, but I did do it. Frankly, that was the easy part. Weightlifting is something I had done in the past, and it felt good to get back into familiar territory.

I was forced to go into a new direction with my finances. With a divorce looming in the future and less than satisfactory compensation at my job, what were my options? I was in my fifties and knew enough about jobs in my industry to know it would be difficult to make a move and expect to come in at a major financial jump. I also knew I could not sustain the level of independence I needed with my income alone and whatever settlement I had from a divorce. I had to find something else and soon! Having health insurance coverage and a retirement account were non-negotiable, so just quitting and making a blind leap of faith was not an option for me. I had only one solution—that is a solution that we all need to have. Multiple Streams of Income, MSI. I needed to have my own business along with my current job.

This is when the tag team for Fear and Self-Doubt came for me. I now knew the direction I wanted to take, but how could I get there? What business could I start? I only knew what I had done as a career. What could I possible do and who would be my clients or buyers? Why would anyone listen to me or give me a chance? Is this something I really want to start at this age in my life? How much money will I need to get started? And, finally, what happens if this does not work out?

These spears and more were tossed at me as I made my decision that this is what I needed to do. My "Whys" gave me the strength to not let these thoughts deter me. Ultimately, I made the decision to push forward and see where this path would lead.

Finding my resources

To proceed, I had to determine who I was in the process. There were so many options for businesses that I first had to narrow down what I was willing and able to do. This is where the fun began. As I stated earlier, there were several people in my circle who were entrepreneurs. One of these people suggested that I attend a conference designed to help and inform attendees of the business opportunities that are out there. Attending these conferences were crucial to my decision to continue this path. The first one I attended showed me that this could happen for me! Information from the next two conferences gave me the idea of the option I wanted to try, e-commerce through Amazon.

As I gained momentum to start my own Amazon sales, I also started to network with people I met at these conferences. On a side note, it was through this networking, that I was able to secure consulting work in areas that were within my skills set. In fact, I have found that networking is an absolute for success. It is through networking that I have been able to have access to knowledge and resources to continue this journey. As I made the decision to pursue Amazon sales, Google and YouTube became my go-tos for additional research. You see, it is one thing to decide you want to sell something, it is another thing to know what that will be. Always present are fear and self-doubt to tell you why you cannot do it. Research and knowledge were the armor I needed to fight back the fears.

I finally had the "perfect" idea for my Amazon sales. It was going to be great, so many would love the results, it was relatively new and would be a success—or so I thought.

Challenges and disappointments

My first venture soon turned into a disappointment as it went nowhere. Having started on this entrepreneurial path, I saw that it worked for others and was determined for it to work for me. Initial failure and disappointment have been in the storyline of many great successes, so I was not deterred. Back to the drawing board and to a new idea, e-commerce through Shopify. Again, I had a great concept and again lack of success. Research and another conference helped me to see things in a more realistic light. I had attended a Shopify conference in Chicago and had my idea evaluated by experts on the platform. While they liked my idea in general, they asked a question that made me change direction nearly entirely. The question was, "Is what you are going to sell represents who you are?" In general, is this me and my passion? The answer was no, not in its entirety. I had to take a true look at what my passion was and then redirect my efforts.

What was my passion? What could I speak to and promote that I could openly demonstrate to others? Then it hit me, fitness. Why in the world did I not think of this before? I had to change direction and go with what I know and what I was continuing to experience and grow in, personal fitness and self-confidence. I had spent years getting to a physique that I was no longer ashamed of. I had seen not only improvement in my body, but in my health and emotional well-being. For some reason, my weight loss had caused me to no longer have the allergy symptoms I had developed—no more numb arms when I woke. I had more energy. I was getting back to my original self, and I loved it!

Where do I go from here?

Now that I have recognized my passion, I am on a journey to share it with others. My life still has many challenges that I am experiencing. This leads back to a question at the start of my story. Are these and have these challenges been a blessing, or if I am just constantly overcoming unfortunate and inevitable barriers to happiness?

They have been a blessing. With each challenge, I have become stronger. I have learned so much throughout this journey, that for me, is just the beginning.

The steps I took to *Take Life by the Horns* were to:

1. Acknowledge and accept that a problem existed.

2. Make a steadfast decision to make a change.

3. Determine my "Why's" so that I had the guidance to get started and keep going.

4. Make decisions. Eventually I had to take a first step.

5. Utilize research, network, attend conferences, and workshops—anything to gain knowledge.

6. Exercise the art of flexibility. Change directions as many times as needed.

7. Document my path. I used it to remember the reasoning past decisions and to help avoid repeated mistakes.

We all have the power to "Take Life by the Horns".

POWER MOVES:

- Be willing to make the hard decisions.

- Know your 'Why"—seriously!

- Recognize if, and when you are spiraling out of control.

Eboni Isaacs

Eboni N. Isaacs is a 25-year veteran Licensed Cosmetologist trained by The United States Trichology Institute and certified by the American Medical Association as a Hair Loss Practitioner. She owns and operates Studio 33 Haircare and Restoration Salon/Clinic in which she herself in caring for her clients/patient's hair and scalp needs. Backed by her faith and extensive training she provides life counseling and healing touch therapy. Ms. Isaacs is the CEO of the Non- Profit Organization, "Moving Star Academy", where the building blocks of personal power are taught and imparted into those who seek to add value to themselves and gain the courage needed to "show up" boldly in life.

Early in life Ms. Isaacs was drawn to the freedom of artistic expression. She trained in ballet, the flute and percussion. Dancing and music are still a vital part of her life as she dances to the beat of her own drum.

Beyond the Border
Believe and Behave Bigly

Eboni Isaacs
Studio 33 Haircare and Restoration Salon/Clinic, Owner

> *"I had to make my own living and my own opportunity. But I made it! Don't sit down and wait for the opportunities to come. Get up and make them."*
>
> **Madam C.J Walker, American entrepreneur**

Life happens to you whether you want it to or not. Sometimes life shows up and kicks you right between the eyes. I am here to tell you that it is not what life brings your way, but how you respond that can describe you as BIG.

Bigly is a word I use to describe who I am and what I do. It is how I show up in the world. "Bigly" is actually "a thing".

I once was described by a native of Africa as a "Big Girl." When I asked what that meant, they explained that because I was very attractive, confident, well-dressed, owned my own home, vehicle, and business, I would be considered "BIG" in Nigeria. Months passed and I was told by this same person to "lower my spirit". At first, I was insulted but quickly recovered and suggested they raise their spirit to match mine. You see, I could have taken their advice and became sub-leveled to my true self to make that person more comfortable. But instead, I concluded that the level of my spirit is what got me to the place of "BIG".

Join me for the next several minutes as I lead you down the path I chose to believe and behave bigly. Are you ready? OK, let's begin.

I. Health- The state of being free from illness or injury. I believe we are spirits having a human experience. You see, to have the best possible experience, we need to nurture the mind, body, and spirit. Maintaining good health can be challenging at times. It is up to you to do the work in obtaining and maintaining your best health. Once you become an adult, the ball is in your court. Here are some ways to stay healthy.

Meditate... Think deeply or carefully about something. This practice is the start of being intentional. It can also allow you to become a less shallow person. Meditation adds depth to your thought process and to your perception of life. This is a way of grounding and rooting you as a more solid human being. It also teaches you to be in the moment. I believe this improves memory because your mind, body and spirit are all in attendance. That makes for a rich moment in life. Would you agree that you are more likely to remember moments of substance? Imagine an upgrade to the quality of your life and memory if your whole being was present every moment of your day. Allocate some time each day to sit and take notice of your breath. Allow your thoughts to wander and then focus on breathing again. Brain-facts.org proposes that "various studies demonstrate meditation can help relieve stress—as well as manage anxiety, reduce inflammation and improve memory and attention."

Hygiene.... Maintain health and prevent disease through cleanliness. By keeping your hair, skin and mouth clean you help to control overgrowth of bacteria. Not doing so presents an unsightly snapshot of yourself. Remember, you do not get a second chance to make a first impression. Too, keeping your means of transportation, home, and workspace clean is very important. It can literally inspire a more positive vibe. Nothing fancy as far as decor...just clean.

Exercise... Any bodily activity that enhances or maintains physical fitness, controls weight, reduces the chance of disease, improves mental health and mood is good for total wellness. For example, dance in your living room, play with your children, grandchildren, or your pets. Take up a sport or walk around your neighborhood. Do what it takes to look your best.

Nutrition.... The process of providing or obtaining the food necessary for health and growth is essential. Do you ever wonder why some days you are more pleasant than others? Your diet can regulate your mood. Eat from the earth and drink plenty of water. It is the key to clear skin, a healthier digestive system, longer life expectancy, and more focused thoughts. Consider how caffeine affects you. How does excessive sugar make you feel 24 hours after consumption? What foods pass through your system easily and what foods do not? Did you know that constipation and dehydration can cause confusion and fatigue and overall bad health? Get acquainted with the relationship between the foods you eat and the response that comes from your body and mind.

Rituals.... This is a series of actions or type of behavior that is performed by someone on a regular basis. On the days I leave my home to show up in the world, I go through a series of acts to prepare myself to engage with others. First, I remember who I am in God. I pray that I stay in character concerning my beliefs. I drink water and clean my body. If going to work, I wear shoes that put me in the mindset of professionalism. When I do not remind myself of who I am or I do not wear my "work shoes", my attitude toward myself is different. Not as bold. Next time you feel good about how you presented yourself and your performance, take note of what you did surrounding that moment. Did you exercise the day before? What did you eat or drink? Was it something that you read? Did you go to a place of worship? Figure it out and duplicate it. If it works again, duplicate.

You have now created a ritual for yourself that will most likely set YOU up to SHOW up BIG. Next, you need confidence....

II. Confidence. A feeling of self-assurance arising from one's own abilities or qualities.

Speak up.... A sign of a confidence is that when one speaks, the volume of their voice is such that the listener has no problem hearing the words being spoken. My mother says she speaks just as loud when she is wrong as when she is right. Although comical, it is a true testament of her confidence. When you converse with others you should be able to hold their attention with the subtle push of power behind your words. Knowing what you say to be true is important also...which leads us to...

Knowledge and wisdom.... Knowledge is acquired through some form of education or experience. Wisdom is the quality of having experience, knowledge, AND good judgment. You know what you know. No-one can take that from you. The knowledge that you have adds value to who you are and who you can become. It is said that "When you know better you do better." It is also said that "Knowledge is power." My understanding is that wisdom helps to apply knowledge where knowledge is needed. So, without wisdom, knowledge is two dimensional...what you know and have experienced. Wisdom adds an element of good judgment. Wisdom gives knowledge the power to influence a better result...Moving on.

Be silent.... Knowing when to be silent is golden. I have learned that being silent at the right time shows your level of maturity. It can preserve your power and strength. If you have already spoken, be confident that what you have stated is enough. Do not over explain. Say what is necessary based on the knowledge you have on the matter and use your wisdom to know when to shut up. When your mouth is shut you can observe and process the situation as well as assess the atmosphere so that you know how and when to move.

Posture.... When it is time to move, make a statement. Posture can describe how you hold your body, and or describe your approach and attitude towards a situation. When I was a teenager, I practiced walking and sitting while balancing a book on my head. This was to train my mind and body to be in alignment so that when I moved, I stayed balanced. The result from this exercise was the appearance of a head held high, shoulders back, and one foot being placed in front of the other to form a vertical line of graceful, confident movement. This came with a lot of practice and tears. My back would hurt trying to hold this form. My natural posture was with a curve in my back and my feet pointed outwards when walking. Also, while looking in a mirror, I practiced what some now call "Serving face". That could mean a pleasant and soft expression, which is for general purposes. Or a fierce, "boss type" of expression with a slight smile—strong, but without the tone of arrogance. The point is to take notice of your body language. When walking into a room of people your posture will speak for you. What does your body language say about you? Show that you are sure of who you are—head up, shoulders back, one foot in front of the other and "Serve Face".

Reputation.... Your reputation is formed by repetitive actions or characteristics. This is how you are recognized by others. A good rule to live by is to treat everyone with respect while maintaining self-respect. This can earn you a favorable reputation that will open doors to opportunities that may not be offered if your reputation is negative. When you have a good reputation you can walk with grace, speak with authority, and share wisdom with confidence that your views are supported by your knowledge. Or, say nothing, and let your reputation speak well of you.

III. Self-awareness. Knowledge of one's own character, feelings, motives, and desires.

Who's in your circle? ... Do the people you allow to be in connection with you on a constant basis include a representative of your past to bring to remembrance of what did not work and measure self-growth? Is there someone who represents your present and hold you accountable? Is there a person you can pinpoint who is positioned to cheer you on towards your goals and your future by sharing their knowledge and wisdom to enhance who you are to become? You also need a hater. A hater is someone who knows your value but cannot help but to display or verbalize their jealousy. Use this person as motivation. Transform their negativity into energy you can use to power yourself to the next level. My advice is to keep your circle small, but each person should have a definite purpose in your life. Recognize and respect their position. Their names may change over the course of time but not the position.

Celebrate small wins.... The success that you achieve will be made of a series of wins and losses. When you experience a "win", no matter how small, celebrate. Show gratitude and share with those who reciprocate love and support you.

Own your mistakes and failures.... This does not imply to allow "losses" to define you. It simply means to take notice and responsibility of what may have gone wrong and the part in which you played. Learn from these experiences and mentally correct the behavior, words and actions that lead to the loss. Acknowledging your mistakes and failures will etch a "Don't List" in your memory for future reference. Treat this list as you would your "hater". Use it to motivate a positive change within you.

Personal power.... "Where human power is sufficient divine power will not intervene" - Rev. Dr Cecil Ferrell. This statement changed the way I viewed my approach to life. I grew up hearing some of my elders say that if the Lord don't do it, it won't get done. But the more recent statement made by Dr. Ferrell implies that we have personal power—power that is vested in us.

And how we use it will determine our destiny. Long story short, I believe I am alive because I spoke life to what should have been a fatal situation. I believed that I would live beyond the border before me, so I proceeded with being proactive in my healing.

Act bold. Fake it 'til you make it.... Seek out what bold looks like to you. You may admire how another person carries themselves or speaks. Apply it to yourself and practice, practice, practice until it becomes a part of your persona. This is not something you broadcast that you are doing. But those paying attention will notice the change.

IV. Discernment and direction. The ability to have good judgement as to what path will be most beneficial is golden. Whether it be spiritual, financial, and occupational path, or choosing whether to continue relationships with certain people, use discernment and direction. Also use discernment when the plans need to change. However, do not abort your mission.

Activate.... Once you have gained mental clarity concerning these matters it is time to activate the plan. Get started. Put your words, thoughts, faith, and expectations into action.

Efficiency.... The ability to produce a desired or intended result. Be productive every day. You may not know exactly what to do but trust the vision, it will all come together.

Momentum.... The quantity of motion that a person or object exerts creates momentum. One day your daily efforts will start to come together, and you will see the fruits of your labor more and more. This is momentum. You are on a gaining cycle. Your health, confidence, self-awareness, direction, and discernment skills are now working in your favor.

Consistency.... Moving in harmony, with regularity. Now that you have momentum, keep it going. Do not let up. Do not allow time to be wasted. Look for encouragement from every angle. If there is no one to encourage you, encourage yourself! Continue self-care in this process. This is BIG! And it is going to take....

V. Courage. One's ability to do something that frightens them. You are on a roll now, but you may have reached your mental, physical, emotional, and financial limits. Push forward anyway.

Fail, reboot, and reload. Expect trouble. Failure. Disappointments. It is okay. Unplug and reboot. Unplug, cut the power source of negativity. Rebooting removes junk in your memory and provides a fresh start or restores you back to a known condition of positivity.... Breath.

Ask for what you want/need. Now you must put your ego, pride, and fear of the word "No" aside. It is time to ask for what is needed to help keep the pace that you have set. This is the time to rely on resources for support. "A closed mouth doesn't get fed." Some of the new information that your resources provide may sound foreign. This is a perfect time to go "Beyond the Border." Stretch out your wings and fly.

Lead.... You have acquired enough valuable qualities to make others take notice of you. To confirm your status of "Big", you are required to teach and lead. This is also where purpose to your life appears. Purpose produces validity. You have earned the right to claim that you "Believe and Behave Bigly".

Power Moves:

- Increase your awareness and resilience to what offends you.

- Be attuned to opportunities and take every one of them that moves you closer to where you want to be.

- Leveling up begins in the mind. Remember, "As a man thinketh, so is he."

CHAPTER 6

Brittany Browne, RN, BSN

Coaching is counseling lit on fire. It is the rare ability to arrive in a life storm of another with a deliberate intent to walk them into their personal arena of sunshine; seemingly unfathomable before. Demonstrating that intrinsic capability with ease is the compassionate professional, Brittany Browne.

Brittany Browne is an educator, advocate, motivational speaker, and highly sought-after Certified Master Life Coach reputed for a sheer excellence in stewarding, inspiring, and delivering practical coaching methods for various audiences. Brittany collaborates with clients in discovering and defining both their personal and professional purpose to achieve goals and unlock the secrets to their own happiness. Having preceded her experience as a Master Life Coach, with an amazing career in Nursing Education, Research, and Quality and Risk support, Brittany has gained the professional clarity in knowing that no two persons are the same and to facilitate growth and transformation, coaching requires personalized, relatable, and uncanny approaches. Brittany's mantra is simple as she takes pride in her communication and organizational skills and understanding its importance for growth and progress. In addition to those values, her down-to-earth style is one of the many traits most appreciated by her clientele and is what sets her apart from others in her field.

Though obtaining her coaching certifications from Transformation Academy, Brittany attests that it has been through the suffering of her own past traumas she is best suited to help her clients. Rebuilding her life after many relocations, marrying in her youth, and losing her mother to cancer all while obtaining a nursing degree in a new place, Brittany realized that deep internal work is required to for self-preservation. This work gave birth to a newer, brighter version of Brittany Browne, leading to the development of Brittany Browne Life Coaching by which she is the founder and CEO. Her services emphasize the power of connecting your past to your purpose and embracing your truth to cultivate meaningful connections within self and others. Because Brittany found her light within, her intentions to help you find your light and to keep your light shining is not only rewarding, itis absolutely necessary.

Swaggin' Your Groove

On Point and On Purpose

Brittany Browne, RN, BSN
Educator, Energizer, Healer

> *"You can never know where you are going unless you know where you have been."*
>
> **Amelia Boynton Robinson, American activist**

A 27-year study found that people with a higher sense of purpose lived significantly longer life than people who do not. In the same study, those lacking an understanding of their purpose developed cardiovascular and gastrointestinal diseases at approximately 2.4 times the rate of those who had already identified and/or was living out their purpose. The influence of social conformity makes people follow the crowd, but each person's journey to and through purpose is unique. Many people miss their chance to step into purpose because they stand on the sidelines and talk about those making moves or decide they should do what others do.

What is swag—what is groove?

For our time together, I want to talk about ways to live on point and on purpose, so you experience your best life *Swaggin' to Your Groove*. The Urban Dictionary defines *swag* as "the overall presentation of oneself." This may include body language, clothing, appearance, personality or energy and the way one speaks. Swagger is the ability to move with confidence and conduct yourself in a way that automatically earns respect. It also shows up with a demeanor of coolness and togetherness. Swagger boosts your confidence walk and increases the odds of instant credibility with people you encounter. It is what sets you apart from everyone else. However, it is not to be confused with cockiness. Cockiness is untamed confidence. Swagger, however, is cool, calm, and calculated confidence. In many ways, it happens naturally.

The term *groove* implies a smooth interaction in business and other situations. It also means to be in a pleasurable place socially or in life. I like to view my groove as my day-to-day vibration while dealing with routines, obligations, and unexpected mishaps. I will use an analogy to better explain. Think of your destiny as a car that is tailor-made for you. You control the car, but you also trust the car will perform as advertised. You expect the brakes to engage and airbags to deploy when appropriate. Having that specific vehicle does not protect you from experiencing inconveniences, such as accidents or maintenance outside of routine services. But for the most part, you trust that the vehicle is safe enough to drive from point A to B. This is groove in action. It is akin to a vehicle tailor made for you. It influences how you show up in the world and move about from place to place.

To be on point is to satisfy whatever is needed for a task or assignment. You think ahead and anticipate outcomes. You make sure to keep a balance between being open to new possibilities and having a plan in the event the situation is no longer favorable. Simply put, you stay ready, so you do not have to get ready. This is fuel for purpose. Purpose gives meaning and direction to life and inspires you to make a significant contribution to the world. To do something ON purpose is to be fully intentional and connecting the reason for which something is done or created.

Look inside yourself for strength

When my 11-year marriage ended in divorce, I was forced to reclaim and redefine my identity. There are many different life circumstances that tend to get us caught up and in a tizzy. However, whether it is an unexpected and/or unwanted break up, the loss of a job, great disappointment, grief, or conflict that seems unbearable, you have the power within to go through and overcome. Grappling with divorce, I was confronted with the realities of life. I started to ask myself questions and quickly realized that my responses were based on attachments to my then-husband. My purpose, somehow in the relationship, had been blurred. I began further investigation of my situation by asking the following questions:

1. What do I like about myself? Beginning with positivity and gratitude opens doors to receive more of what we want.

2. What do I dislike about myself? Knowing this allows you to make changes in these areas.

3. What would I do if weren't afraid? How you answer this question could be lead you to what you really want to do in life. Have you been playing it "safe"? Fear is the most common reason people never step into purpose.

4. As a child, what did I want to be as I grow up? Connecting with your inner child is healthy and highly recommended to live a purposeful life. It is possible that your vision for your future is hidden in those experiences.

5. Am I happy with current job or career? Is it fulfilling? Is there something else I desire to do?

6. What do I worry about the most? You will be surprised at how much stress and anxiety you carry for situations for which you have little to no control. Pinpoint stressors and question them so you can focus on areas you can change.

7. What are my goals for the next month? Year? Figure this out so you can effectively plan and mold your life to achieve short-term and long-term goals.

8. What mistakes do I continue to make? Do I know why I continue to make them?

This process of questioning is ongoing. At times it can bring up negative emotions such as guilt, shame or even anger, so give yourself grace and space to feel, deal, and heal. In some cases, you may not be able to answer the questions, which is okay. Do not be discouraged. If you need time to figure it out, be sure to revisit it later. Remember, you cannot swag your groove or be in purpose if you are not honest with yourself.

Looking inside is a hack to creating inner peace more quickly and authentically. The information you gather can empower your decision making. As you become a better version of yourself, you are better equipped to help those around you do the same. This ultimately creates a ripple effect of positive changes in and around your space. When you are on point and on purpose, you groove in a way that accesses peace, prosperity, and abundance.

As you come into your own, you have an opportunity to determine where you find connectedness. Self-awareness is a combination of how you see and think of yourself in relation to how society sees and thinks of you. Who are you? Here are several questions I explored to reflect on my own self-awareness.

1. How am I different now than 5 years ago? In what ways have I changed or grown? I used to be interested in a lot of social gatherings and events, but now I am more introverted and can appreciate time in solitude. I recognize that being alone is not a bad thing, it is necessary at times to rejuvenate and recharge.

2. What do others say about me that I like to hear? I liked to hear people say that I was down-to-earth and that I am always "doing my own thing". This makes me happy because I have never been the type to follow the crowd or hop on the latest trends. When it comes to being "swaggy" and purposeful, you can't be that if you do what everyone else is doing.

3. What triggers me? I asked this question to help me tap into past traumas or unfavorable situations I had faced. For example, the biggest trigger for me is any sense of abandonment. My father was absent, so my mother was a single parent. Unfortunately, mom passed away with cancer in 2013. Not only did I lack a strong male figure in my youth, but the person I saw as my protector was no longer here on Earth. I learned to suppress sadness at an early age. Anytime someone mentions they are talking to their mom or going somewhere with their mom, I am reminded that my mom is no longer with me.

Experiences have a direct impact on your evolvement. The information you gather should empower you in your decision making. Take the scenic route through self-discovery. Be open to new opportunities and put yourself in places you would usually avoid. Because your beliefs are influenced by relationships, taking an introspective approach will help sort out what originates from within and what is driven by external factors.

Swag and groove are connected to self-love

It takes courage, wisdom, and compassion to fully accept the good, the bad, and the ugly of who you are. Swag (your appearance) that is void of confidence is, well, superficial and empty. To swag, or to show up confidently while grooving (interacting) on point and in purpose, you must genuinely accept who you are and like that girl or guy. Self-acceptance should not be based on your achievements, love life, or social status. You are human and you will make mistakes but be accountable for them and move on. Acknowledge when you make progress towards your goals and reward yourself. A person who has mastered self-love becomes a force to be reckoned with. This individual has a high regard for their own well-being and happiness. If you do not love yourself, it will be difficult to discover love within others. Get in the habit of using positive self-talk and reinforcing the qualities you appreciate by complimenting them. I repeat the following affirmation daily:

Self-love is non-negotiable. Believing in myself increases my motivation and resilience. I have what it takes to succeed. I overcome anxiety and doubts to go after what I want. I am eager to act and seize opportunities. I leverage my strengths. I apply my strengths to my personal and professional life and find new ways to use them. I focus on activities that engage my natural talents. I continue learning to increase my capabilities by adding to my knowledge and skills. I welcome constructive feedback. I accept my feelings while making rational decisions. I test myself by dealing with uncomfortable situations instead of avoiding them. I advocate for myself. I honor my needs and stand up for my principles. I repeat affirmations to fill my head with positive self-talk. I stand up straight, make eye contact, and smile. I project confidence. I am equipped to handle any challenge that comes my way.

Take a moment to reflect on your deepest desires. Create an affirmation that motivates you to live on point and on purpose as you *Swag in Your Groove*.

My affirmation:

Power Moves:

- Be open to new opportunities and put yourself in places you would usually avoid (places with the potential to elevate you, of course).

- Rediscover yourself. Get in the habit of positive self-talk and the practice of self-love.

- Give yourself permission to courageously face whatever is holding you back from being on point and on purpose.

Sharon T. Hoskins, Esq.

Sharon is a skilled matrimonial attorney and certified divorce mediator with over 20 years of experience handling marital conflicts. A graduate of Dartmouth College and New York University School of Law, Sharon has been recognized annually as a NY Super Lawyer and is known for her practical, no-nonsense approach to just about everything. Her tenacity led her to establish Hoskins LLP, a boutique matrimonial law and mediation firm she founded with her husband, Rob Hoskins.

Married for 25 years and mother to three wonderful sons, making her the only female in the household, Sharon is always up for a challenge. She is an avid runner, who loves trail runs and exploring new places. She has completed 16 marathons, an ultramarathon, over 100 half marathons and many other races in 22 states. Her goal is to complete a half or full marathon in all 50 states. As the founding Ambassador of the Black Girls RUN! Long Island running club and a certified run coach, she has motivated many others to hit the pavement and has coached several women to run the NYC marathon. She has recently expanded her athletic pursuits to include swimming and biking to claim the title of Triathlete.

Sharon is also passionate about community service. She is an active and dedicated member of Jack and Jill of America, Inc., where she works with other mothers to develop and implement programs to develop leadership skills and promote community service amongst children and teens. She is a proud Silver Star member of Alpha Kappa Alpha Sorority, Inc. Sharon enjoys singing, dancing, and tackling puzzles and brainteasers.

Are you looking for motivation and support to achieve your goals? Join Sharon's Motivation Nation at www.MyMotivationNation.com.

Mind the Gap

Getting from Where You are to Where You Want to Be

Sharon T. Hoskins, Esq.
Motivation Nation, Founder

> *"Every great dream begins with a dreamer. Always remember, you have within you the strength, the patience, and the passion to reach for the stars to change the world."*
>
> **Harriet Tubman, American abolitionist**

Do you know that only one percent of the population has completed a marathon? That is 26.2 miles of continuous running for at least two hours if you are an elite superstar or closer to five or six hours if you are someone like me, a 50-year-old, overweight, mother of three and self-employed lawyer, who loves to eat. Why would anyone voluntarily choose to put herself or himself through that? In the time it takes me to complete those 26.2—do not forget that .2 miles, you could go see a movie, have dinner, and take a nap before I even cross the finish line. I think people who run marathons are a little crazy. The good kind of crazy—the kind of crazy that compels you to dream big, take chances, do the unexpected, and experience life fully. It is that same brand of crazy that gets you to take the leap to get from where you are to where you want to be. With courage, preparation, determination and faith, anything is possible. You can DO IT[3]!

Dare to achieve. Organize a plan. Immerse Yourself. Take action. Taste Victory and Thrive.

Be a goal setter

Let's talk about Setting Goals. We often talk about our dreams, hopes, wishes and aspirations. *I wish I could lose weight. I hope I win the lottery. I dream of traveling abroad. I want a new job.* But, do you ever take the steps you need to get on the path to achieving these dreams or do you remain satisfied with keeping them as mere fantasies? How many times have you said I wish I could win the lottery but do not ever or rarely buy a lottery ticket? While the chances of winning the lottery are very small, it most certainly will not happen if you do not get a ticket!

Let's look at something more achievable like travel. Have you looked up a specific location you want to visit? How much is the flight? When is the best time to go? What are the options for lodging? Once you do the research to determine the cost of the trip and the best time to go, then you can work on how you will pay for such a trip. Calculate how much you need to put aside and for how long. Determine your vacation schedule at your place of employment. These are all concrete action steps that will get you closer to your goal of making that trip you dreamed about become a reality. If you want to do it, then DO IT!

Dare to achieve, Organize a plan, Immerse yourself and Take action, Taste Victory and Thrive.

Anything you want to achieve requires action. Forming a plan and taking the right action increases the likelihood of success.

Truth, dare, and consequences

The first part of any journey requires a recognition and acknowledgment of where you are in the moment—an introspective self-assessment. A truth-telling. The more honest you are with yourself, the better able you are to plot out the necessary next steps and prepare for your next move. This notion is not news to anyone. Most are familiar with the 12-step plan of Alcoholics Anonymous. The organization's mantra is, "The first step is to admit you have a problem." This idea calls for honesty about your current condition. That admission is your starting point. This is who I am now and that is who I want to be in the future. It is all at once a statement of realization, affirmation, and defiance. I am not who I want to be...yet. I want more!

Three words—*I want more*. It takes a certain amount of courage to make that declaration, to say aloud. This is not enough. I want more. I am reminded of that scene from the Charles Dickens novel, *Oliver Twist*, where the poor, orphan boy, Oliver, finishes his bowl of gruel (porridge) and, still hungry, makes his way past the astonished faces of the other orphans in the workhouse to the stern cook. He had the audacity to say: "Please Sir, I want some more". No other orphan boy had dared ever ask for more. Prior to Oliver's courageous declaration, the boys had drawn straws to determine who amongst them would take that bold action. For so long, their fear of the consequence of such a declaration silenced and paralyzed them to accept the status quo of their hunger and weakness. Why didn't all of them rise and demand more? Surely, they are stronger together. Instead, they remained fearful and weak.

Oliver chose the short straw, accepted the challenge, and with courage took the step to declare "I want some more." Notably, he said "I", not "we". He stood alone in his declaration. Alone, he dared to take that first step. Perhaps that scene is so memorable because it resonates with each of us in some way. That fear of what will happen if you voice your desires can be overwhelming. That moment when standing alone you speak up and declare a goal, a purpose. It can be frightening. Will others laugh at you? Scorn you? Will you get any support or be left to deal with the aftermath on your own? If you fail, will everyone see you as a failure? Is it even possible to succeed? Do you have what it takes? One seed of doubt can stop you dead in your tracks before you even begin. Doubt can be so powerful that you start to form excuses to justify your doubt and fear as valid reasons not to move forward.

When I first had the notion to consider running a marathon, I had many doubts and a lot of fear. I ran track in high school and had always dreamed of one day running the NYC Marathon. However, it had been 20 years since my high school track days. I was not a very good athlete then, so I had very low expectations of any athletic ability when I was pushing 40. Additionally, after having three children, I was about 30 lbs. overweight and was not physically active at all. I was as an associate at a boutique law firm specializing in divorce law, working long hours in a highly stressful environment, dealing with clients going through the most difficult time of their lives. Outside of my legal career, I was also very involved in my community, serving as PTA President at my sons' school, singing in my church choir, and serving on the executive board of a family-focused community organization. My plate was already full, but with all of this going on, I still wanted more.

I wanted to lose weight and improve my physical fitness. These were not unique goals. Exercise and losing weight are the most common New Year's resolutions year after year. A 2014 research study by the University of Scranton revealed that 25% of New

Year's resolutions are forgotten or dismissed within the first 2 weeks. After six months more than 50% have given up on their goals. By the end of the year only 8% have completed their goal.

This desire for something more occurred around 2008 when the *Biggest Loser* was a hit show. A friend of mine decided to put together a Biggest Loser Challenge. Twelve of us would pay an entry fee and weigh in every month for three months. The person with the highest percentage of weight loss would win the pot of money. This challenge sparked the competitive nature in me and became the impetus for my running journey. I knew the monetary prize was not enough to keep me motivated. I needed a more unique goal. I thought about that dream I had to run a marathon. A marathon? At the time even the thought of it was too big for my brain—too much of a dare. I took that honest self-assessment of my level of fitness, or lack thereof, and adjusted my goal to what I felt was still daring but more realistic and achievable. I decided to train to run a half marathon—the Long Island Half Marathon to be exact. I knew the training would naturally cause me to lose weight and then I would have a good chance of winning that Biggest Loser challenge and the prize money. Triple motivation!

So, I accepted the dare to achieve something more, something great. I declared my goal to friends and family. Once I put it out there, I knew I could not back down. I am not one to quit; I rise to a challenge. Putting it out there made me accountable. If I had kept it to myself, it would have been too easy to find an excuse to quit because no would know about it. Although, making a somewhat public declaration was a bit scary, it was also exciting and even empowering. No one I knew at the time had run a half marathon. I felt bold and courageous about the challenge of running 13.1 miles, even though I could not even run 1 mile at that point.

My friends did not laugh at this crazy idea of mine. Some did show skeptical surprise but not enough to be discouraging—more of a wait-and-see what happens kind of attitude. Others were supportive and helpful. My husband was my greatest supporter.

So now that I declared this goal, how would I ensure that I would be a part of that 8% who achieves success?

Organize a plan

Preparation is key to everything. There is a famous quote by Benjamin Franklin that says: "if you fail to plan, you are planning to fail". I wanted a plan for success, not failure. A study by Professor Gail Matthews, a psychologist at Dominican University of California, revealed that people who write down their goals are 20% more successful in accomplishing them than those who do not write them down. Moreover, those who set up action steps and do regular progress reports to another achieve 40% more than those who do not. Effective preparation requires thorough research, a written plan with clear measurable tasks, and accountability.

I did not know the first thing about running a half marathon. I also did not realize there was so much to learn. I had to do a lot of research. I scoured the Internet for training plans. I read articles about running, how to get started, what shoes and clothing to wear. I chose a beginner training plan that started with walking and gradually built up to running more and more.

I incorporated the training plan into a calendar so that I could easily see what I was supposed to do for each day of the week. This allowed me to check off each day's work out as I completed it. I could easily see the progress being made. I consulted my run calendar every day to make sure I stayed on track with the training plan. That was my accountability.

Social media can also be a great accountability tool. Posting regular progress reports on a Facebook or Instagram page helps to keep you motivated and allows others to send you messages of support and encouragement. Other useful methods of accountability include joining a support group, identifying an accountability partner to work with you, setting a regular schedule and sticking to it.

An effective strategy is to incorporate accountability milestones. These are opportunities to celebrate small successes and share those achievements along the way to your goal. Reaching each milestone is great motivation to continue the journey. As part of my training plan, I signed up for races of shorter distances to measure my progress. Not only was I keeping myself accountable, but I discovered a whole new world of people, places, and events that I never even knew existed—and it was fun! I was able to learn a whole lot more about the sport, the running community and race events in my area and out of state. It helped to enhance my preparation and training because I was able to talk to others who were knowledgeable and share experiences with those who were on similar journeys to mine.

An additional key part of preparation and planning is identifying and gathering all the supplies and equipment needed. That list of supplies should also include resources, which can be books, websites, blogs, clubs, people—anything or anyone that can provide information and inspiration for you. It is important to determine the types of equipment, tools, and gear, that are appropriate for your needs at the time. I recently started working towards another goal of completing a sprint triathlon. As a beginner, I do not need that beautiful lightweight titanium bike that costs over $10,000 when a $500 bike will work fine for my current level.

Immerse yourself

You have done your research, collected information, written your action plan and gathered your resources and supplies. It is time now to fully immerse yourself into the plan and invest the time and effort to see it through. Immersion will help to keep you motivated. Surround yourself with people who have similar interests. Join a group or club around that interest. Become a member of a Facebook group—there are a plethora. Go to the places and events that others with similar interests frequent. The camaraderie will serve as another source of support and accountability for achieving your goal. When possible, carry out parts of your plan with a partner. Inevitably you will help push each other. There is an African proverb that says: "If you want to go fast go alone, but if you want to go far go together." Use others to motivate you and create your own community of support.

When I decided to run this half marathon, I subscribed to running magazines, websites, and blogs. I joined a running club and went for some of their group runs. I learned about the best websites to purchase goods at a discount. When I visited the local running store, I talked to the salespeople, who were very helpful and full of useful information.

I stress the importance of finding a support network because sticking to a goal is hard. It requires determination and fortitude. The strategies suggested here will help you. Write down the action steps, post it where you will see it regularly, gather all your tools, check off completed tasks to stay accountable, celebrate the small victories, create your own support group, jump in all the way. There will be moments when you may get sidetracked or momentarily deterred. Life happens. That is okay. Adjust and get back on the plan. Do not beat yourself up about a minor setback. I cannot speak enough about what how helpful a support group or partner is to keep you going.

It also helps to find a mantra that resonates with you and motivates you to keep moving toward that goal. It can be as simple as one word—Go! I use that one all the time when I am running and feel like I am losing steam. It can be a corny phrase, a song lyric, a quote—anything that lights you up. It does not have to be the same mantra. There may be different ones that you use for different situations. Whatever it is, claim it as yours and use it to get you through the rough patches. Visualize yourself completing the goal you set, review the action plan, adjust as needed and immerse yourself back into it.

Take action – follow through

You must DO IT! Be Daring, not doubtful; Diligent, not daunted; Determined, not deterred. Declare success. Take ACTION. I talked about having a mantra to help get your head in the right space and to manage your mindset. However, the most important thing is to take physical action. Get out of your head where doubt and fear like to hang out. The physical manifestation of each part of your action plan will lead you to completion of your goal. Do not just visualize the goal, cut out or draw a picture of the goal. Create a vision board that you post somewhere in your home where you will see it every day.

Do not just make a mental note of things that you think you need to do towards the goal. Write out the plan, step by step, with timelines and specific tasks that are to be done. Vague notions are not sufficient. Set reminders on your calendar, tell a friend to nag you. Post that plan on social media so that you feel a sense of responsibility to follow through. Change I want to I will to I did. Acknowledge each milestone along your journey and capture it with pictures or write about it in a journal.

When you complete that goal savor the victory. Reward yourself—you earned it so make it good. You deserve it. Then...set another goal and DO IT again!

Taste victory and thrive

Training for my first half marathon was a long nine-month process. On race day in May 2009, the weather was warm but
there was a steady rain for the entire race. The rain reduced
the number of spectators that usually gather along the route
to cheer on the runners, so it was a little lonely in that regard. I
swear they moved that last mile marker an extra mile down the
road because it was the longest mile ever. I remembered my
mantra—Go Sharon Go—and pushed through to cross that finish line. I did it. I completed my first half marathon...in the rain!
And, remember that Biggest Loser Challenge? I lost a total of 32
pounds and WON the challenge and the cash!

After finishing that first half marathon, I set a new goal to complete the full marathon at that same race the following year. I
found a marathon training plan, put in the work, and finished
my first full marathon in May 2010. Since then, I have run a total
of 16 marathons, including four NYC marathons, over 100 half
marathons, and a 31-mile ultramarathon. It is amazing what can
happen when you follow through on one simple goal.

Start now. You never know where the journey will lead next.

POWER MOVES:

- Dare to stretch your current reality.

- Live by the declaration of "I want more".

- Reward yourself for progress as well as accomplishments.

72   The Power of **Bold**

Eileen Cooper Reed, Esq.

Eileen Cooper Reed is a change maker and advocate who currently resides in Cincinnati. Her entire adult life has been dedicated to the improvement of the human condition particularly for children and families of color.

Before becoming a lawyer, Eileen trained in community development and worked in both rural and urban settings. During law school, she honed her technical writing skills. After graduating from the University of Cincinnati College of Law, she did a stint at the US Court of Appeals before settling in as a Juvenile Court Referee.

In 1993, Eileen opened the Cincinnati office of the Children's Defense Fund. Her passion and dedication for improving the lives of our most vulnerable children and their families was exceptional and eventually she assumed the helm of the Ohio office of CDF.

Eileen's devotion to service led to her election to the City of Cincinnati Board of Education where she served two four-year terms. Addressing the issues of equity in education and in other sectors throughout the community became a driving force. While on the Board of Education, Eileen was elected to the Executive Committee of the Council for Great City Schools, the preeminent organization committed to urban education. At CCGCS, she chaired the National Advisory Committee on Black Males.

Since her tenure on the Board of Education, Reed founded the Intersections Group which purpose is to advance conversations that matter: acknowledging and examining the intersections of racial equity in community.

Did you know:

- Eileen and her husband Jim have 17 grandchildren.

- As a teen, Eileen grew up at the Ohio State Reformatory for Men (where her father was warden).

- Eileen's parents were both identical twins whose identical twins also married in a double wedding

Audacious Faith

Restoring Hope in Dark Times

Eileen Reed, Esq.
The Intersections Group, Founder

> *"If you lose hope, somehow you lose the vitality that keeps life moving, you lose that courage to be, that quality that helps you to go on in spite of all."*
>
> **Dr. Martin Luther King, Jr., American minister**

Some days it feels like the world has gone mad. Turn on the tv or any media outlet, for that matter, and the constant barrage of negativity and confusion overwhelms you. Sometimes you feel like you just cannot breathe.

Dark times, you say? The last year, 2020, qualifies as one of the darkest. The emergence of the Covid-19 virus and its fast spread across the planet was so frightening. The numbers of infected Americans grew exponentially while information about strategies to address the virus were often conflicting and certainly disturbing. Increasing cases and a significant number of deaths from Covid-19 left most of us reeling.

Very quickly, those employees who could were directed to work remotely whether they were computer savvy or not. Frontline workers everyone depended on still had to show up to work at great risk to themselves. We were told to wear masks, wash down everything in our houses with alcohol—that flew off the shelf—and to keep a social distance of six feet. Mostly, people just stayed in the house if they could. Soon, schools were closed, and businesses were closed, and millions of workers were laid off or otherwise terminated.

Our institutions felt like they were crumbling. The public schools were ill-prepared to teach virtually or to provide the technical equipment and resources all students needed when the pandemic began. Some parents had to make the choice to leave their jobs to care for their children. Hospitals were overrun and health care workers contracted the virus in record numbers. Protective equipment was nowhere to be found. The world seemed to be collapsing around us.

And, as if the death and devastation from the virus were not enough, May 2020 brought us an event that was unspeakable. On a street in Minneapolis, police arrested a Black man named George Floyd and when they finished with Floyd, he was dead. The entire incident was videoed and the whole world saw the breath drain from his body. Protests were sparked around the world as people watched a police officer kneel on Floyd's neck while he cried, "I can't breathe." Weeks and weeks of demonstrations occurred across the cities of American and in other countries.

If you do not feel like these were truly dark times, the tragedies and hardships of everyday life were added to the havoc caused by both Covid-19 and the continued police brutality against unarmed Black people. Joblessness, food insecurity, other sickness and death, and the lack of childcare loomed as an additional shadow over our communities. In the midst of this chaos, we have each needed to decide our response in these dark times, these times which seemed to take our breath.

Because of the stress, fear and anxiety caused by the environmental and societal conditions, some have simply given up. Overdoses and suicides have risen sharply. These folks have little hope that things will get better. Others get depressed and may be generally unable to function. Yet another group operates in confusion, not able to take confident steps forward. They seem powerless to decide in which direction to go. And, finally, there are those who have been intentional in their discernment.

And so, how can you determine a way forward in a time that feels so heavy that you may not want to move? Where can you find the strength and courage when it seems like all is lost? How can you restore hope in dark times?

Faith is the way

"Now faith is the substance of things hoped for, the evidence of things not seen" (Hebrew 11:1). This verse informs you in the first instance that faith and hope are inextricably linked. But "faith is a tricky thing, isn't it? Believing in what you cannot see," says Reverend Karen Wylie in the *Science of Mind Magazine, May 2021*.

Every day, I recite a Twelve Power meditation. The first affirmation is about Faith. "My faith moves mountains inside and out". The doubt that can confuse you comes from either internal sources or external ones. This last year has provided lots of things outside of you to react to: the virus and the illness and death associated with it, the racial reckoning, trauma, and heartache attached to it, and the very personal tragedies that you experienced. Internal sources included the fear and doubt that arise in you and the anger you feel at the unfairness of it all, and perhaps, your inability to do anything about the way things are.

So, how do you muster the faith necessary to "move" those mountains? The faith we speak of has two basic aspects: trust and belief. Trust means that you accept that there is a power greater than yourself operating in the world. That divine essence exists everywhere, including inside of you. And no matter what is going on— "the craziness, the confusion, the fear"—you trust that you can rise above it.

Belief, on the other hand, means that you firmly embrace the notion that all things are possible.

Weaving together trust and belief in your divine light is the basis for having faith to embrace that which you cannot see. As Corrie ten Boom, Dutch writer says, "Faith sees the invisible, believes the unbelievable, and receives the impossible."

Hope lifts you up

Though faith is the substance, hope is the motivator. These two virtues are typically spoken of in the same breath because they operate in tandem. Hope is that light at the end of the tunnel. That light is the divine light which is also the basis of your faith. Light is the unconditional love at the heart of all life, the basis for all good. Being aware of the love in you reminds you of what is possible and gives you the strength to keep moving forward despite great disappointment.

The hope we speak of here is more than the mere expectation or wish that something good will happen. "Hope isn't naively denying the problem. It is relentlessly believing in the existence of a solution". And that solution springs forth from the unconditional light and love in you and is securely grounded in your faith.

Audacious faith: One woman's story

You sometimes hear about people taking large leaps of faith. What prompts them to do so? Usually, some big problem or "dark time" confronts them, and they must decide how to respond—how to see their way through.

Let me tell you about Carolyn. Almost 25 years ago, my friend began having problems with her eyesight. She thought all she needed to do was to go to her optometrist and get a new prescription and a new pair of glasses. Much to her surprise, Carolyn was diagnosed with a benign tumor on her pituitary gland that threatened her eyesight. She had no idea what to do and was at her wits end.

Another friend told her, "Carolyn, there's a blessing in this situation for you if you are open to it." So, she began more fervent prayer and meditation, gave thanks for the blessings, and opened to the possibilities. Soon thereafter, Carolyn's doctor told her a new procedure had been developed that treated pituitary tumors like hers. And even better, the doctor who developed the procedure had begun to frequent the city where she lived and was willing to do the surgery and do it quickly. Carolyn was told that doctors and others came from around the world to see the surgery performed.

The surgery was deemed a success. Still, some of the tumor was left on her gland and her doctors recommended radiation to shrink the remainder of the tumor. This story was not yet over.

Carolyn had another decision to contemplate—radiation or not? Once again, she heeded the question of her friend and looked for the blessings in this difficult situation.

Carolyn requested a picture of the x-ray of the tumor on the gland. She posted the picture in her bathroom where she could see it every day. She announced to the doctors that she would not be engaging in a radiation regimen saying, "The God that makes the sun rise every day and I can take care of this tumor." Carolyn said that affirmation every day, sometimes several times often waving her hand over the picture. When she visited her doctor several months later, the doctor reported that the tumor was gone. It had disappeared. The medical personnel had no scientific explanation for the cure. They were as astounded, and Carolyn was as grateful once again. What better display of audacious faith than Carolyn's?

After fear reared its ugly head when she was diagnosed, she was soon drawn back to the blessings that were hers to acknowledge. The new medical procedure, the doctor who developed it, even the proposed radiation regimen, all these things were vehicles of hope for Carolyn. Her faith was clearly expressed, and the outcome was a much-needed healing. Her faith can be called audacious because she chose to take a leap of faith in her treatment that was quite bold.

Hope revisited

Take one more look at hope before you see how this might work for you. An old Chinese proverb suggests, "As long as we have hope, we have direction, the energy to move and the map to move by." The direction comes from hope being the light at the end of the tunnel. You will always be drawn toward that light and see the steps you need to take in getting there. Having hope does not mean that there are not disappointments along the way, that there is no doubt or fear. Hope does mean that, like Carolyn, there are real ways to create solutions.

Dark times to hope—how to get there

The dark times of the last year and a half have been perpetuated by the media's constant and repetitive bombardment of information and disinformation. There are lessons you can learn from Carolyn's story about how to deal with them.

The first thing to do is to unplug—the more the better:

- Turn off the TV, including the news.

- Pause to answer the phone—especially when you sense the perpetuation of bad energy.

- Put the newspaper down for a minute.

- Allow yourself to be still.

- Listen to soothing music.

- If you meditate, take some time to do so.

Remove toxicity as much as possible. Remember that light within you? Dwell on it. Call to mind the blessings you experienced in the last year. Take time to be grateful and appreciate them.

Recently, I had a bout with breast cancer. The oncologist suggested a lumpectomy and after several rounds of questioning, I decided to do it. Then, she suggested a course of radiation as a preventative step to recurrence of the cancer. I was less receptive to this proposal. I complained to several friends that I was not sure I wanted to "Injure myself on a daily basis." Then, hearing the complaint, one friend said, "The radiant light of Spirit is healing you now." What a difference that prayer made. I said that affirmation every day during my treatment. Embracing the small change of mind and heart allowed me to see the radiation for the treatment it was, and I was able to express my gratitude. I experienced no side effects from the radiation of any consequence.

The acknowledgement of the blessings is the light that appears at the end of the tunnel. Developing the muscle to make this shift takes practice. Light provides the direction for you to move. Light always shows the way to go. It is the hope of possible solutions. In his 1647 writing of *The Mistress*, Abraham Crowly notes, "Of all ills that one endures, hope is a cheap and universal cure."

Faith will see you through

While hope is the virtue that motivates you to move, faith compels you to do so. Helen Keller, American author wrote, "Faith is the strength by which a shattered world shall emerge into light." How Keller, a person who was rendered blind and deaf as a child could go on to graduate not just from high school but from Radcliffe College with honors is astonishing. Though her life was shattered by blindness and deafness, Keller's faith gave her the strength to achieve things others fully able did not. She became an advocate for the differently abled because of her audacious faith.

In these tumultuous times, we can all stand some audacious faith. And if you simply look, you find those rays of hope: the unusual verdict of guilt for the officer that killed George Floyd; the development of several effective vaccines to combat the pandemic swiftly, and the reconnection of families who had not spoken in quite some time. If you look to the light, you will always move in the right direction. Then, with faith, you can breathe.

Power Moves

- Sweat the small stuff—acknowledge God in small and big blessings.

- Take a break from the fast pace of the world—slow down to get ahead faster.

- Hold on to hope.

84   The Power of **Bold**

Alicia Delgado-Gavin, PsyD

Dr. Alicia Delgado-Gavin has spent over 17 years working in the social services field assisting clients with a gambit of behavioral and mental health disorders. Educated at Hofstra University, Dr. Delgado-Gavin specializes in marriage and family relationships, suicide prevalence, domestic violence awareness, and empowerment.

Dr. Delgado-Gavin loves to provide individual and family counseling services and facilitate seminars where she encourages others to seek help when needed. She supports others in identifying unhealthy relationships, identifying when they feel mentally unstable and how to get help.

In addition to private counseling services and speaking at seminars, Dr. Delgado-Gavin is the author of the book titled, *Tears Behind the Smile*, which is based on her personal experience as a survivor of domestic violence. She believes that people need to be heard but have a hard time acknowledging and expressing how they feel. Dr. Delgado-Gavin provides people with tips and positive coping strategies to combat trauma, especially those who have experienced domestic violence. She encourages others to pray, meditate, journal, seek counseling and speak out to help build strength. These are some of the techniques that she used on her journey to healing.

Dr. Alicia Delgado-Gavin loves to empower others and provide people with a sense of hope, peace & joy. With all that she has been through and all that she is working towards, her biggest motivation is her family. Dr. Delgado-Gavin is a wife and a mother of four. Her family is her biggest support system, and they inspire her to continue promoting mental health wellness daily. She maintains peace and stability in her life by praying daily, focusing on self-awareness, and practicing self-care.

Failing for Success
Turning Defeat into Victory

Alicia Delgado-Gavin, PsyD

Psychologist, Licensed Marriage & Family Therapist, Speaker

> *"Bringing the gifts that my ancestors gave, I am the dream and the hope of the slave. I rise. I rise. I rise."*
>
> **Maya Angelou, American poet**

Have you had a dream, or wanted something so bad that you would do anything to obtain it? Have you ever worked hard for something, but things just seemed not to go right, and it appeared as though everything you were working towards was a failure? Well, I can attest that the past 14 years of my life have been nothing short of a journey filled with upsets, rejections, and failures. I must thank God that I am here and able to talk about my trials and tribulations and tell my story.

Growing up I received a lot of love and admiration from family and friends and was encouraged to strive to be successful. From the age of sixteen I knew that I wanted to be a therapist and make a change in the lives of others. I was passionate about my career choice and willing to put in the work to achieve my goals. However, the journey to make my dreams come true was met with so many unimaginable obstacles that broke my heart and spirit and I almost gave up on myself. But thankfully, God never gave up on me. Today, as I reflect on that journey, I know that all those setbacks and obstacles were necessary to prepare me for success and to remind me to never forget where I came from.

Do all you can do – then trust

After I graduated from high school in 2002, I went to Pennsylvania State University and majored in psychology and sociology. During my four years away from home, I worked three jobs and completed my internship. My goal was to get into a doctorate program right after undergraduate school. I worked hard to make sure my work experience was superb, I took the GRE, which is the Graduate Record Examination, and submitted my resume and course curriculum to five major doctoral programs. After doing all this, I did not get accepted to any of the schools. I was devasted. Thoughts kept running through my mind as to why I was not good enough, what could I have done differently, and why this was happening to me. I felt like a complete failure. I then decided to get my master's degree in marriage and family therapy, work as a counselor at a girl's detention center and then reapply for the doctorate program.

I had a plan—and I was going to make sure I sought that plan through. Unfortunately, my plan was not in alignment with the path I was headed. While in the master's program, I gave birth to my daughter and my son a year later, which were both unplanned. The pressure of trying to be a full-time graduate student, young mother and girlfriend to a man who offered little support, took a major toll on my health. I became so sick that I had to drop out of the master's program. In my mind I thought I would take off a semester to get myself together. But before I knew it, eighteen months had flown by, and I still had not reenrolled.

During those months, I finally had the nerve to leave that abusive relationship with the father of my children and was forced to work two jobs to take care of my family. All the while my heart ached because I was incomplete inside. I wanted to go back to college and finish what I started but I had lost my way. The pain was more crushing because some of the people I thought had my back started doubting my ability to finish school. I allowed their words to manifest in my spirit, which led me to doubt myself. I became resolved to stay in that desperate place and live with the hand fate dealt me. And then one day as I was driving home at 1:00 am, after completing my waitressing shift, I had a breakdown. I did not recognize it at the time, but it meets the criteria for a breakdown for sure. I cried uncontrollably because I had fallen so far away from my dreams, and I did not know how to get back. I felt like a complete failure. But then I heard a soft voice in my head say, "Call the school and finish what you started."

> *"Two things in life that leave and never return, Time and Opportunity. Make sure to seize them both"*
>
> **Anonymous**

After months of working multiple jobs, completing an internship, being a mother to two very small children, and building a new relationship, I graduated with my master's degree. I felt amazing. I felt as though everything was looking up for me and I was finally on the path to success that I had envisioned as a young girl. Little did I know that moment would be short lived, and I would be back in a dark place where I could not escape. All that hard work meant nothing, so I had thought.

Beware of the curveballs – they will come

In 2014 I decided to go back to school to become a doctor. One of the best decisions of my life, but one of the most stressful times in my life. My husband and I were both working great jobs and expecting our first child together. Things seemed to be going well but then I had to resign from my state job due to the conflicting schedules between school, work, and internship. We were nervous about bills getting paid but assured each other that things would be ok. I took comfort in knowing my husband was working full time.

At the start of 2016, my husband was preparing to graduate with his master's degree, and we were getting ready for the birth of our daughter. It is crazy that when things seem to be moving forward, a curve ball always gets thrown in the mix. My husband was laid off from his job two months before the birth of our daughter. At this time, we had three children, rent to pay, two car notes and the revolving bills that had no mercy on our situation.

After my husband graduated, he was having a hard time finding a job in his field. He worked part-time and took care of the children while I worked part-time, attended my internship, and went to school. We used all our savings and lived on credit cards to survive. During this time, we were so deep in over our heads, that we could not see a way out. Asking family or friends for help was not an option because they were dealing with their own life stressors. We had to grudge through and do what we could.

During that time, my car was repossessed, and we were facing eviction. I felt defeated. I thought, can things get any worse? My will to keep going had dwindled and I was so hurt and devasted that I could not utter a prayer out of my mouth. One night, as my husband and I sat in silence for about two hours, we began talking about our living situation and possible things we can do to get out of this situation. We had no tangible solutions. As we sat on our bed, with tears rolling down our cheeks, we kept asking ourselves, "How did we get to this place"? I felt sad, angry, and embarrassed, but I knew I was not going to let this break me. I grabbed my husband's hands and said, "Lets pray". At first, we could not even get a word out. Then as we cried out to the Lord for guidance and an answer, I began to feel a strong sense of peace.

The power of prayer

Most people do not understand the power of prayer. I am a true testament as to how prayer saved me. My husband and I found a place to live, and I graduated with my doctorate degree in 2018. I was now a mommy of four, a doctor, and ready to put my plans for success back in motion. As my husband and I started writing down and manifesting what we wanted and needed to be successful, things started happening for us. We began to connect with people who encouraged us; people who did not question or doubt our goals. We started generating multiple streams of income and finding peace within ourselves. Looking back at all that I had been through, I now realize that the things I went through were the catalyst for me to be the doctor, therapist, motivational speaker, author, mother, wife, and woman that I am today. All my failures pushed me into my destiny and my future of success.

Through it all, I never lost my faith in God. I learned that nothing in life is a given. Working hard to achieve your dreams makes the victory even sweeter. All the things that I thought had defeated me, turned into my VICTORY!

Power Moves

- Accept that setbacks and obstacles are necessary to prepare you for success.

- Give thanks in all things. God works *all* things together for your good.

- Do not underestimate the power of prayer.

CHAPTER 10

Wendy Labat, DBA

Dr. Wendy Labat, *The Financial Healer*, is an award-winning entrepreneur, business strategist, international speaker, and two-time best-selling author. She is the CEO of The Financial Cures LLC, and creator of **The Financial Cures System™**, a results-based program for financial mastery. Dr. Labat is the producer and host of the global streaming production of "***Financial Cures with Dr. Wendy.***" She has her Doctor of Business Administration (DBA) degree in Entrepreneurship and over 37 years of experience as an entrepreneur.

Dr. Labat shares the knowledge, experience, and wisdom garnered firsthand from the challenges she faced starting a business 37 years ago, with no business experience, limited financial resources, and most recently conquering breast cancer. This journey led her to develop **The Financial Cures System™** (TFCS). She has improved the financial lives of many entrepreneurs, business owners, families, and individuals across the U.S. using TFCS™.

Dr. Wendy wrote the #1 New Release book, ***Diagnose Your Financial Health*** to get people started on their journey to optimize their financial health. She empowers her clients to formulate specific strategies to diagnose their financial health; take control over their finances; make their money work for them; acquire proper protection to prevent financial ruin; build a financial legacy; create generational wealth; and become financially free to live the life they desire.

In addition to being one of the authors of *The Lemonade Stand: Book 2*, Dr. Wendy Labat has been featured in many publications such as *Success Profiles Magazine, Authority Magazine, Lemonade Legend Magazine, Black Enterprise*, and *The Atlanta Tribune* to name a few. She is featured in the *50th Anniversary PBS American Portrait* broadcast. Furthermore, Dr. Labat was inducted into the *Marquis Who's Who* as Top Entrepreneur/Business Owner.

Roar

How to Prevent Financial Ruin

Wendy Labat, DBA
The Financial Cures System™, Creator

> *"There is a difference between being broke and being poor. Being broke is a temporary economic condition, but being poor is a disabling frame of mind and a depressed condition of the spirit."*
>
> **John Hope Bryant, American entrepreneur**

Life is unpredictable. You plan for your personal and business goals, vacations, daily activities, and other objectives that you want to achieve with the assumption that everything will go as outlined. In the back of your mind, you know that something could happen to interrupt your plans, but keep those thoughts buried with little or no consideration of alternatives to the "what if" scenarios.

When one door closes, another one opens

God has a way of opening doors, revealing opportunities, and weaving valuable lessons into what seems to be the difficult, disappointing, and worst times of your life. Let me share with you how God used these times in my life to redirect me to opened doors of opportunities, revealed progressive strategies, and valuable lessons that empower me to be successful as I continue my journey to fulfil the calling on my life to secure my financial future.

Over five decades ago, I set out on a journey to become a medical doctor. I completed high school in 3 years and college in 4 years to get an early start on my medical training. While attending undergraduate school, I landed a position in the laboratory at a major healthcare facility. This was my prerequisite to get ready for my future medical training. I learned a lot about medical technology and was paid extremely well. Things were going well.

There was never a doubt in my mind that I would not achieve my career goal. I strategically planned and executed what was required to get to the next level of my journey. All my education was centered around science. I had no desire to pursue any other field outside of medicine, so I did not take any courses outside of my pre-med major to prepare for an alternative career.

Rejection letters began to come in from the medical schools. I was totally devastated when a major door was slammed in my face as I received the final rejection letter. I was not going to medical school. There was no plan B because becoming a medical doctor was my only career goal.

My alternative at the time was to pursue a career as a research scientist or get an MBA. I went on to graduate school to get an MBA with emphasis in Healthcare Administration. This was a good alternative career choice, so I thought. Near the end of the program, one of my professors told me that I needed a mentor to become a healthcare administrator, because positions at the top were limited. He stated that the current hospital administrators had proteges' they were grooming to move into positions once they retired.

Without a mentor I was left to fin for myself. Furthermore, when I started the MBA program, hospitals were nonprofit, highly regulated entities. By the time I received my degree, hospitals became non-regulated, for-profit entities, advertising discounted rates for certain surgical procedures to fill hospital beds during low occupancy periods. Everything I learned in graduate school no longer applied in the real world. Again, another door closed to my new potential career.

These closed doors seemed like devastation and wasted time. I did not understand why these disappointing events kept happening to me. My youth, limited perspective, and unwillingness to veer away from the plans I set for my life, blinded me from understanding how the process worked to discover the call for my life. Little did I know that God was teaching me valuable lessons as He redirected my path to fulfill the calling placed on my life. Each time a door was closed, a new opportunity was presented.

The opportunity to teach at the college level was presented to me. The salary was excellent for the time required and I would be able to continue to work in the laboratory. The money I was making was more than I had ever made but I did not feel fulfilled with either of my career choices. Making a lot of money was a priority because of the financial goals I was trying to achieve, but there was still a void in my professional life.

An adventure of a lifetime came when I moved to Sicily, Italy. This opportunity was exciting and scary at the same time. In preparation for the move, I began to study the Italian culture and language via home study courses. Once I relocated, I relied heavily on my self-taught version of the language and an Italian dictionary as I ventured out daily among the locals. I landed teaching positions at two U.S. universities' European divisions and was paid extremely well. After two years, an unfortunate incident occurred and I was forced to move back to the U.S., with spur of the moment planning and preparation.

My return to the U.S. landed me in the South, with a warehouse job for a major corporation that required manual labor and paid much less than I was used to earning. I was discontented with the physical labor and wanted to quit, but after three days I was offered a promotion to a position in the payroll department. The pay was still considerably less than what I was used to making but it was an increase from my warehouse wages. My duties in the payroll department exposed me to how payroll was managed and how office politics worked in a major corporation. After several months in that position, I grew tired of the monotonous tasks.

Management thought I would do well as the assistant supervisor of the accounts receivables department and offered me the position. The offer came with a higher salary, still not commensurate with my previous salaries before returning to the U.S., but more than the payroll position. My professional and management skills were beginning to shine as I discovered several areas that needed improvement. I developed solutions to increase productivity, efficiency, and cost savings in the department, so the company implemented the programs I developed.

The company comptroller began to include me in the fiscal and developmental meetings and asked for my input in planning future budgets and programs. I was getting excited about my newfound career and the contributions I was making to the company. The accounts payable manager was leaving the company and her position was going to be available. The manager of my department expressed an interest in that position. She was about my age and was going to junior college to get a degree. She had been with the company since high school. I expressed interest in her position to the comptroller who would make the final hiring decision. I thought I had a good shot at the position, especially since my solutions had improved the company's bottom line. Additionally, I had an MBA degree.

Life changes when least expected

Things were beginning to look up for me professionally, or so I thought. A department meeting was being held to announce who would fill the account payable manager position. I was expecting my manager to be named to fill the position. Instead, the comptroller announced that the management of the Accounts Payables and Receivables Departments was being consolidated into one management position and that my manager would be the new manager over both departments. Another devastating disappointment and a bitter taste of corporate politics.

After the announcement, I decided to take a leave of absence to look for another job. While reading about a local, young, successful entrepreneur in a premier business magazine, I imagined a career in sales but did not have any sales experience. The excitement about the possibility of entering a new profession grew stronger. I contacted the gentleman I read about in the magazine and applied for a position as a sales rep with his office equipment company. He hired me immediately.

The commute to the office was about 40 miles each way as well as travel around the city to meet with potential clients. The sales manager promised to train me on the products and take me out on sales calls. He assigned me to a few clients and gave me leads to follow up with. After my first week on the job, I was told that I would have to go it alone because the sales manager had resigned. So, I set appointments for the week and went out alone. Things were going well; I even made a few sales with the limited training I had been given. An emergency sales meeting was called. We were notified that the company was bankrupt and that we were not getting paid.

This was another devastating experience because of the expenses I incurred with the 80-mile daily round trip commute, plus driving the additional miles within the city, all while depleting my savings. Meanwhile my previous employer informed me that if I did not return to work from my leave of absence, they would consider it as a voluntary resignation. There was no doubt in my mind that I was not returning to that job regardless of my current situation. I informed them that I was not returning and that they could consider it whatever they needed to consider it as.

One of the other salesmen offered us an opportunity to come work for him at his new office equipment company and get paid the money that we were not going to receive from the bankrupt company. Of course, I agreed because I really enjoyed my new profession as a sales rep, even with the uncertainty of working for the brand-new company. During the transition from the bankrupt company to the new company, I gathered the names of clients, vendors, and leads to use moving forward. The new owner kept his word and met the payroll from the previous company. Another closed door led to a new opportunity.

After about a month, my new employer stated that he was moving the company to Florida. He offered us our positions if we were willing to relocate. I had just returned to the U.S. less than a year before and did not know anyone in Florida, nor was I willing to relocate. The closing of yet another door.

Not knowing what to do, I spoke with my father about the situation. We decided to start our own office equipment company. My father was a teacher and had less business and sales experience than I did. He was not giving up his teaching position but agreed to be the figurehead of the company. His lack of understanding about business caused us to part ways soon after the formation of the business.

Here life goes again

Entrepreneurship was never a consideration as a career goal, but I enjoyed my experience as a sales representative with the previous companies. I ventured out totally on my own after my father and I parted ways from our short-lived business venture. My solo my entrepreneurial journey began. I opened my own office equipment company with no real business experience and very limited financial resources. This was a time when there was no internet or social media, and the only thing you could do with a cell phone was make an expensive phone call.

My clients were major corporations. To be considered for the big contracts, my company had to project the right image. That meant having a brick-and-mortar office, employees, inventory, and all the overhead that goes with it. If you projected anything less, your company was perceived as a mom-and-pop operation not capable of handling the big contracts. Of course, I went after the big contracts. At first, I was not making any money and struggled financially to keep my head above water.

These were challenging times. The more sales and contracts my company acquired, the more inventory had to be purchased to fulfil the contracts. The payroll, rent, utilities, and other expenses had to be paid along with the cost of the increase in sales regardless of my cashflow situation. Times got tough because my cash flow did not match the growth of my company. The fact that I loved what I was doing so much outweighed my financial challenges. My limited financial resources forced me to think outside the box to meet my expenses and cashflow needs.

This experience taught me how to take control over my finances; make my money work for me; negotiate with my clients to pay my company invoices sooner rather than later; negotiate with my suppliers for better pricing and payment terms. I continued to find creative ways to acquire the things needed to improve and increase the growth and development of my company.

Eventually, I got out of the office equipment business and opened a tax preparation company. The tax preparation business was very lucrative. I had no intentions of going back to school for another formal degree. A few years later I enrolled in a Doctor of Business Administration Degree Program with emphasis in Entrepreneurship. This move was in response to the prompting of the Spirit.

In 2014, when the Affordable Care Act mandated that everyone have healthcare coverage, I expanded my tax preparation business to include insurance products and financial services. Not wanting to be a hypocrite, I believed if I was going to sell my clients these products and services, I needed to acquire them for myself and my family. So, I purchased the products I was selling and sharpened my financial services skills. This move was done as part of a business and marketing strategy, not from a personal financial planning perspective. I did not think I would have to use any of it.

In 2016, one of my colleagues had a routine physical and was notified that he had kidney cancer. I expressed my concern about his diagnosis but indicated that he was going to get a significant influx of income because of the products we sold. He indicated that he did not have any of the products he was selling and would not receive the influx of income it could bring. He did not practice what he preached.

In 2017, I was notified that the results of my semi-annual mammogram required that I have a biopsy to test a growth that showed up on the image. A couple of days later I underwent the biopsy. I had already decided that if the results were positive, I was going to do everything to nip it in the bud. The radiologist told me the results would be back in about 3 days.

Three days later I called the radiology department only to be told that I would have to get the results from my doctor. When I called my doctor's office to get the results, I was told that I would have to schedule an appointment to get the results. I told the receptionists that I wanted to schedule an appointment to get my results. She put me on hold for about 3 minutes.

Eventually the office manager got on the line and told me that the doctor does not make appointments to discuss test results. I asked her how I could get my results. She said that I could come by the office and pick them up. I immediately drove to the doctor's office. When I arrived, I was handed a sealed envelope with the results of my biopsy. I went to my car, opened the envelope, and read the results. I saw the word "carcinoma" and knew that meant I had breast cancer.

A sense of peace came over me. I did not cry or panic. I had no clue where to go from there, but I knew that I could not go back in that doctor's office to inquire about my next steps when she would not even show me the professional courtesy of telling me I had breast cancer. I became furious but knew I did not have time or energy to waste on her lack of concern or professionalism.

I sat still in my car and asked God for direction and was led to call a friend who was a breast cancer conqueror and explained my situation to her. She gave me her oncologist's phone number and told me to call her office. I called the number, explained the situation, and was told to fax my biopsy results to the office. Within 5 minutes of faxing the results, I received a call back. The person on the phone asked for my personal and insurance information, which I happily provided. She told me that they did not accept my insurance but said she would call me right back.

About 10 minutes later, she called back and gave me the number to a local cancer center at a major university in the city. She told me to call them right away because they were waiting for my call. Sure enough, when I called, they took my information and scheduled an appointment for me to see an oncologist 3 days later.

In the meantime, I did all kinds of research about breast cancer. I did not know anything about the disease other than what I had seen on TV commercials for various breast cancer drugs. Nobody in my family had breast cancer. My friend, who was a breast cancer conqueror, inquired how things went with her oncologists, and invited me to her home to discuss the matter. I asked her to tell me about her experience. Not only did she share her experience with me, but she also showed me the scars from her botched reconstructive surgeries.

This caused me to do even more research about the types of breast cancer, oncologists, surgical oncologists, types of chemotherapy, facility, and the treatment and surgical options available. I wanted to be prepared for my appointment with the oncologist so I could ask questions and make informed decisions about my course of treatment for the disease.

During my visit with the oncologist, she thoroughly explained the type of breast cancer the biopsy revealed. She stated that I had the most aggressive form of breast cancer and provided me with various treatment options to fight the disease. I chose the most aggressive form of treatment.

I was near the end of my Doctoral program when the chemotherapy started to really take its toll on my body and mind. My body was in an extremely weakened state. I looked like a bald-headed skeleton with a layer of skin over it. I literally had no fingernails or toenails and was suffering from a severe case of chemo brain. God gave me the strength to see me through the program to complete my doctoral study, oral defense, and walk across the stage at the commencement ceremony to become Dr. Wendy Labat, with my family and friends in the audience to cheer me on as they had done throughout my journey battling breast cancer.

Blessed by financial cures

My chemotherapy infusions were every three weeks for a year at a cost of $67,000 per infusion, which totaled over $1.1 million. Additionally, I had 5 surgeries, multiple CAT scans, MRIs, ultrasounds, mammograms, and lab tests that exceeded a cost of $300,000. Can you image having to pay those kinds of medical expenses in addition to your personal and business expenses while battling breast cancer?

The cost of treating this disease could have ruined me and my family financially. Thank God I practiced what I preached. My health insurance paid all my medical bills. Plus, the supplemental coverage I purchased paid me a significant multiple six-figure tax-free payout that allowed me to focus on my recovery without worrying about money. I considered this a financial cure.

After completing all my treatments and conquering the disease, I was healthy, wealthy, and happy in my comfort zone. God had other plans for me as He had throughout my life. He told me that He brought me through my journey better than I started. And hence, The Financial Cures System* (TFCS) was developed to empower others to prevent financial ruin.

Subsequently, I began my crusade to improve the financial lives of many entrepreneurs, business owners, families, and individuals across the U.S. using TFCS*. Furthermore, my clients become empowered to formulate specific strategies to diagnose their financial health, take control over their finances, make their money work for them, acquire proper protection to prevent financial ruin, build a financial legacy, create generational wealth, enjoy financial freedom, and live the life they desire.

Are you a faithful steward over your finances? Many people think getting more money will be the answer to all their problems. In reality, understanding how to manage money, no matter the amount, and making money work for you is the real solution. If you do not manage and control what you have now, how will you manage and control more?

Most people keep a written record of their income and expenses but overlook tracking their spending. Uncontrolled spending can prevent you from paying for the essential things you need, reduce/eliminate debt, build an emergency fund/cash reserve, and become financially free. Detailed tracking of your income, expenses, and most importantly, your spending helps you ascertain a realistic picture of your financial situation.

The objective is to plan where your money goes instead of wondering where it went. To achieve your financial goals, you must know your current financial situation. Once you have a realistic picture, no matter how good or bad, it takes three essential elements to move forward. You must decide, commit, and take action to achieve your financial goals. Your mindset and discipline require the transformation of your thinking and habits as they relate to your desired level of achievement. You cannot want a rich man's wealth and have a poor man's mentality.

Many professional women and entrepreneurs are responsible for the financial well-being of their businesses and families. It can be a struggle if you do not have the mindset, knowledge, discipline, and tools to take control over your finances and make your money work for you. My Best-Selling #1 New Release book, **Diagnose Your Financial Health,** was written to empower people to overcome the obstacles to winning the money game and achieve optimum financial health to become financially free to live the life they desire.

Evaluate your journey to optimize your financial health by taking a realistic look at your financial condition and finding the right prescription to cure your financial ills whether it involves anorexic income, overweight expenses, obese debt, or a spending addition. Learn how to optimize your financial health regardless of the current economic conditions.

What could have been a medical and financial disaster turned out to be a medical and financial blessing. A business strategy and a breast cancer diagnosis led to my discovery of the "financial cure for breast cancer;" formation of The Financial Cures LLC; and creation of The Financial Cures System ™(TFCS). I am on a crusade to empower others to diagnose their financial health. take control over their finances, acquire the proper protection to prevent financial ruin, build a financial legacy, create generational wealth, and enjoy financial freedom to live the life they desire.

One illness or injury can limit or end a person's ability to earn an income. The interruption of income, continuation of personal expenses and addition of mounting medical bills increases the likelihood of bankruptcy. Properly protecting your health, life, finances, and legacy can safeguard your money, prevent worry, reduce stress, and provide financial peace of mind that enables you to focus on your recovery.

My life's journey took various twists and turns. My life's goal was to be a medical doctor, but God had other plans. He closed doors, revealed opportunities, and taught me lessons that prepared me to follow the path the Spirit was leading. His calling on my life was for me to become a doctor, not a medical doctor but a Doctor of Business Administration and be "The Financial Healer" to those who suffer with financial illness.

Power Moves

- Diagnose your financial health – this is vital to your overall wellbeing.

- Know that your wealth is connected to your health. Behave as if this true because it is.

- Appreciate and learn from every season of your life.

CHAPTER 11

Yvette Vega

Yvette Vega is the Director of Public Relations Neurobehavioral Research, since 2006. Some of Yvette's responsibilities include developing strategic partnerships with medical centers and liaising with patients, family, and the clinical team. Her most important function, however, is outreaching to the medical community and informing them about alternative approaches to wellness. Vega has worked on over one hundred psychiatric research protocols, all approved by the FDA. Her experience includes schizophrenia, major depression, borderline personality, PTSD, and bipolar disorder.

After work hours, Yvette invests a lot of her time into fitness. She believes fitness can help people tend toward stability and peace in addition to the health benefits it provides. Yvette is herself a fitness certification specialist, trained oriental dancer, and hula performer and yoga instructor who has helped many people reach their goals. To further promote wellness, Yvette filmed an award-winning documentary, *Courage and Healing Death,* to help individuals cope with traumatic experiences in their lives. Vega is the creator of the *Endorphins Mind Body* system.

I Will Survive

Thriving After Loss of Thyself

Yvette Vega
Endorphins Mind Body System©, Creator

> *Someone once asked me the meaning of unconditional love.*
> *I looked at my mother.*
>
> **Author unknown**

My hopelessness and desire to live had thoroughly metastasized. The notion of navigating through life's existential perils had become too daunting for me. I wanted to die. Suicide adulation, self-loathing, and chronic insomnia. In one thirty-day period I hardly slept at all. Restlessness had become my constant companion. In falling into such a depth of depression, I was keenly aware that my poor and rapidly declining mental health was adversely affecting my physical health. Here is the thing though: I no longer cared.

Hopeless and deflated

"Do you feel as though life is still worth living" is an often-repeated question posed by the mental health care clinician to the depressed patient. The question is posed to assess whether a suicidal intervention is warranted. To which most would respond, "Yes, life is worth living". This would likely be your answer despite some of you having had thoughts of taking your own life, if you were honest—but for the fear of purgatory or other unknowns. In reciting his soliloquy, Shakespeare's Hamlet contemplates a self-inflicted departure from his life. Waxing dramatically about being in a deep state of depression, he speaks about "...the thousand natural shocks that flesh is heir to...." However, he temporarily reverses himself by pondering what may, or may not, await him in the afterlife. That pretty much summed up my life. Like Hamlet, I was tired of living. However, due to unresolved mental trauma that stemmed from the sudden death of my sister when I was a young girl, and the perceived paranormal occurrences right after the death of my mother, I was afraid of dying.

Still, a constant state of deep depression consumed my will to live. While living with the stifling emotional pain, emptiness, and feelings of hopelessness that come with depression, I became very adept at going through life's motions. I hold a promising career in Psychiatric Research, hosted a television program, and became a highly sought-after yoga teacher for almost thirty years. Outwardly, I had achieved what many would have considered to be a rousing success. But I would have gladly traded those outward appearances of success for being able to feel normal again, to love again—to live a life without being burdened with the constant constraints of mental illness.

The solemn purpose for telling my story is to give you a sense of what it was like to be afflicted with a deep mental depression, all the while struggling daily to hide the inner turmoil and pain, to appear to be the high-functioning person that so many had erroneously perceived me to be. My clinical depression began as a pre-teen lasting almost unabated way into adulthood. There were also cultural impediments in my young life that staved off real treatment. My family members, like so many others, had a general lack of knowledge of what a real depression looks and feels like. So that discussion is warranted here.

My spiraling into a deep-dark depression was precipitated by the death of my mother. But a clinical depression that extended way beyond the normal bereavement period had been an earlier visitor in my younger life with the death of my sister. When my older sister passed away at twenty-three from a cerebral aneurysm, my twelve-year-old world was suddenly shattered. The specter of death being so up close and personal was a foreign concept, one that my preteen aged mind had not yet learned to grasp. I was her baby sister, the youngest sibling of the lot. She had shown me a world beyond dainty white first communion dresses, candy apples, and fastidious penmanship. I admired and looked up to my mother, but it was my sister's tutelage that I believed would guide my exploration into young womanhood. And just like that, without any preexisting medical condition, she was gone.

Facing life without my sister had become too daunting. I became so emotionally crippled that for weeks I refrained from speaking to anyone. My poor mother was saddled with the grief of losing her beautiful young daughter who had just blossomed into womanhood, and at the same time effectively losing her twelve-year-old one, who became all but mute. This strong matriarch who instilled principled life-long lessons and wholesome values in which to live by into all her children was now rocked by the loss of a child and threatened with the loss of another one. She did not know what to do. She tried her best to keep me from falling into the abyss.

Hope and healing

From my early teens up until four years ago, my mental state had gone from a protracted bereavement and clinical depression to a full-blown psychosis. Long-term psychological therapy was of little help; and because of a pre-existing medical condition, antidepressants, or psychotropic drugs were not an option for me. Thus, the barrier to sound mental health seemed insurmountable four years ago.

The consensus among many mental health professionals is that young girls are more susceptible to being plagued with depression than young boys, so it may appear from the narrative that some of the depicted issues that were symptomatic of my depression was somehow gender specific. I do not believe this to be totally correct. Thus, as I relive on these pages the episodes of being psychologically broken, it is my hope that male and female alike can arrive at a better understanding of what it is to be clinically depressed and to seek professional remedies for such a malady before all hope is abandoned.

After years of self-reflection, which my condition steadfastly resisted, I was most fortunate to have found my mental health remedy. And just like that, while in the depths of my despair, a lifesaver appeared. He was/is a big guy with light hazel eyes and has the comportment of a clumsy adolescent. Besides the unconditional caring he shows towards me, he sheds on my couch and suffers from bouts of way too much flatulence. He is aptly named Star, a four-year old Alaskan Malamute, my emotional support animal who became a trained Psychiatric Service Dog.

There are distinct differences between an emotional support dog and a psychiatric service dog. An emotional support dog is a pet that provides comfort or emotional support to a person. Unlike a service dog, an emotional support dog does not need to be trained to perform specific tasks.

A psychiatric service dog is trained to recognize and respond to its handler's disability by performing specific tasks. The handler must have a mental or psychiatric disability that limits one or more of a major life activity, like suffering from Major Depressive Disorder. More so than the emotional support dog, the psychiatric service dog is protected by the ADA to virtually all public access, anywhere its handler goes.

It is not always easy to obtain a psychiatric support dog. However, if you are a sufferer of depression, post-traumatic stress disorder (PTSD), getting a psychiatric support dog may be right for you. To qualify for a service animal, you need to get written documentation from your healthcare provider that you have and are being treated for an emotional or psychiatric disorder or disability and require the assistance of an animal because of it. The work a dog has been trained to do must specifically relate to your condition. Training a service dog yourself can be difficult and can take years. Usually, you would get a service dog from someone else who has already trained it.

Before getting any kind of pet or service animal, it is important to seriously consider the responsibilities that come along with it. Think about whether you can care for it physically, mentally, and financially. Service animals are a big commitment. And every landlord (or co-op board in my case) does not allow dogs. But that can be circumvented—with varying degrees of difficulty—if your professional health care provider certifies your need for a service dog.

If Star Vega, my Psychiatric Service Dog could talk he would say:

'Sometimes my mom sleeps a lot, so I worry for her. But she takes amazing care of me; she cooks for me almost every day. On those occasions when she cries, I snuggle up to her and sheepishly give her my paw, which I learned to do in psychiatric service dog school. When she is feeling well, she is fun to be around. We do things like go on adventurous hikes. She even takes me to agility classes. It keeps me focused on the many tasks that I was trained for. And get this, When I am not working, I go to doggie daycare and get to play with some of my pooch friends. When I first came into mom's life, I was an emotional support animal. But when I discovered how much mom needed

me, I went for additional training at Paws of War and became a psychiatric service dog. I know that my mom needs and depends upon me. I love her very much.'

These days my roaming thru pet supply stores and spending funds freely multiple times a month have become ritualistic. Star is the sole beneficiary of all those pesky canine toys and tasty doggy edibles that I buy. I do not complain. Although his veterinarian (or my accountant) would hardly approve, weekly truffles washed down with a splash of champagne would not be too good for him. That would be the least I could do; because in coming to my emotional rescue four years ago, he literally saved my life.

"Man can live about forty days without food, about three days without water, about eight minutes without air, but only for one second without hope."

Anonymous

Power Moves

- Be strong enough to admit when you are weak. This is the character of strength.

- Identify what you need from yourself and from others.

- Recognize both your limitations and resources.

Kendale M. McDaniel (Ken Diesel)

Ken Diesel, WMQ, is a decade long fitness professional, nutrition coach, and training facility owner in Fort Myers, Florida. Diesel is a decorated Army Special Operations veteran, and 2-time brain surgery survivor who brings a fiery blend of uplifting energy and honed training to his specialized fitness courses. He is the father of 5 beautiful children, and the lucky husband of Rosie.

Cut Loose

Count Your Loses and Calculate Your Next Moves

Kendale Diesel
Fully Armed Fitness LLC, Owner

> *"For the Word of God is alive and powerful. It is sharper than the sharpest two-edged sword, cutting between soul and spirit, between joint and marrow. It exposes our innermost thoughts and desires."*
>
> **Hebrews 4:12**

Cut it out...

I could hear it as if it were yesterday. The wails were a cry of desperation for relief from agony. It would not go away and there did not seem to be a simple fix for my distress. Pouring tears, scratching, and clawing at my own scalp, I was an utter mess. The adversarial 'IT' was a cyst. More specifically, a left ventricular arachnoid cyst approximately the size of a softball. Nothing mattered more than getting that little piece of adversity out of my head. Little did I know at the time, I would endure another eleven months of the same, excruciating symptoms before experiencing the relief I was seeking from the first of two brain surgeries.

You win some, you learn from some

We all love winners! Nearly all of us can identify with the joy that victory typically brings with it, and satisfaction of triumph after conquering the opposition. There is, however, something that is particularly inspiring and enthralling about a victory attached to an unblemished record. Sports fanatics seem to carry a special place in our memories for the undefeated. As a self-proclaimed sport enthusiast, I can recall many championship seasons. However, an undefeated championship season tends to spark a luster of its own. The '72 Miami Dolphins, the '95 Nebraska Cornhuskers, the (02-03 & 10-11) UConn Huskies, and the '09 'Bama Crimson Tide are just a few sportsman's examples of how a 'perfect' record enroute to championship gold has inspired many fans like me.

Much like winning seasons, a losing streak can also spike memories and conversation. The biggest difference is often a solemn and begrudging mood sensed in a loss. After listening to hours of after game interviews one thing is evident—players and coaches would much rather cut a loss and calculate their next move towards more victorious outcomes. If only this were simpler?

But, what if you could simply 'cut loose' every loss, and every save face instance of your life? What if you could just do away with the traumas that have accumulated over the years? What if the number in your "L" column, on the right side, was a zero—and remained that way throughout your life? At first thought, it may be difficult to imagine yourself absent of adversities that have led to the exact point you are right now. Heck, you may even be knee-deep in some challenges as you read this, but please allow me to encourage you—the problem is hardly ever the problem. Rather, your response to the problem often becomes the issue to overcome.

Win – 0, Loss – 1 from the start

I ran and won many races before this race. As a Florida All-State competitor, I held several school records during my high school tenure. The University of South Florida signed me to an academic-athlete scholarship and in the first season of track and field, I was named Freshmen Athlete of the Year for the team. Life, my young life, was all well—until it was not. At the tender age of 19, as a sophomore athlete life presented a hurdle that would take several years for me to clear. At the finish line of a 4x400 high hurdle relay run is where the discovery of my 0-1 record began. In what would be my last track and field meet, after more than a decade as a competitor, I collapsed just past the finish line, completely disoriented. Vomiting, dazed, and confused, I was rushed to the hospital for immediate care. My mother, there to cheer me on at this 'home' track meet, looked on in horror as the paramedics drove away from the field to get me to the university hospital emergency room.

It was there in the emergency room, alert but weakened, that I received the news of what I would later spend waking nights crying, screaming, and pleading to desist. After a CT scan it was revealed that I had a softball sized cyst pressurizing my left frontal lobe. Unbeknownst to me or my parents, the cyst was a congenital birth defect—something I had since before I was born. And if this was not enough of a shocker, soon after this blow to my winning season, the attending physician asked me, with my mother close by, the most layered and introspective question I had been asked to that point in my life. I still remember the tone of his voice, "Did you ever incur any trauma or a traumatic event in the womb?"

My mother is the most resilient person I know. That night when I was diagnosed with a brain cyst, we cried together in what was one of our all-time closest moments. I witnessed her not just survive or endure but *conquer* and emerge stronger from an abusive marriage to my father. Memories of getting ready for school, watching my mother covering the physical and emotional wounds left behind by a husband-figure who put his hands on his wife in anger remain fresh in my mind. It was if he was justified, or if it was okay. I would go to school, and she would work hours after these seemingly endless violent episodes, like nothing happened. In one of our most emotional conversations in that tiny hospital room, I discovered the sorts of violence she experienced, and I with her, while I was in her womb. Though we did not speak about the moment of awkwardness when the physician posed that question, I think we both had suspicious ideas about what may have happened to cause the cyst. In my mind, I was diagnosed with a direct manifestation of the exact chaos I spent most of my life desiring to be free from—the hands of domestic violence as a young child.

> *"For God has not given us a spirit of fearfulness, but of power, and of love and discipline."*
> **2 Timothy 1:7 (ERV)**

Though your win-lose experiences will be different from mine, you will pass through disappointment and experience the pain of temporary defeat. Life happens to all of us. What experiences have taught me is that I, nor you were designed to set up camp in the loss column. Downfalls are not my, nor your identity. However, unfortunately for many people, that is *exactly* what happens when downfalls find a permanent home in what is only meant to be a temporary space in the mind or soul. When you accept defeat as a part of your identity, it is as if you are *clothing* yourself with its effects that manifest like a thick wool coat. Now, coming from a native Floridian, I am sure you can imagine how useless this type of garment would be for most seasons throughout the year. And that is not to say that defeat cannot serve a powerful purpose, just as a heavy wool coat may very well have its viable uses in one's life. But in this example, a wool winter coat can do quite a bit more than outlive its purpose by the time you are encroaching upon the spring and summer of your life. The same thing that brings warmth and relative comfort, if worn for too long and at the wrong time, can and will become burdensome and overbearing if it is not properly removed. Defeats can manifest a very similar effect if they are not released in a proper perspective. A loss can serve as a learning point, turning point, and steppingstone in the winter seasons, seemingly defeating times.

> *"I never lose, I either win or learn"*
>
> **Nelson Mandela**

One of the more effective protocols I had the honor of implementing during my service in the United States Army Special Operations Command was the After-Action Review (AAR). We incorporated this protocol into virtually every important aspect of our performance in the military. In this stage of my life, I have found it to be an invaluable spiritual tool as well. First used by the Army on combat missions, the AAR is a structured approach for reflecting on the work of a group and identifying strengths, weaknesses, and areas for improvement. It has helped me to maintain a system of checks and balances when considering my win-lose columns.

A proper AAR is centered around four questions:

1. What was anticipated to happen?

2. What transpired?

3. What went well, and why?

4. What can be improved upon, and how?

AARs serve as phenomenal tools for leaders to actively assess an event, adapt to mistakes, and overcome future events of similar nature. One of my favorite aspects of a proper AAR, is how it never concludes with shortcomings or defeats, but rather a call to action of correction. When we consider the effect that wallowing in defeat can have on your psyche and spirit, then it may be easier to consider how unphysical our encounters really are. Ephesians 6:12 in the King James Bible reads, *"For we wrestle not against flesh and blood, but against principalities, against powers, against the rulers of the darkness of this age, against spiritual wickedness in high places"*. By the time my tenure in the U.S. Army had come to an end, I realized just how powerful, and spiritual an AAR can be, if applied consistently through my life.

"Your loss column isn't the problem—it is your attitude about your loss(es) that is the problem"

Ken Diesel

By now you may have already succumbed to a loss or two. If you are still reading this though, it is not too late to seize victory. The amazing feelings I remember from my early days of performing AARs that persist today, are the emotions of victory, triumph, and boldness. AARs have a magnificent way of taking the sting out of defeats. Nothing says victory like a defeat. Yes, you read that correctly, nothing reveals victory like defeat.

Looking back on life circumstances, I am grateful for many of my perceived losses. In the middle of struggle and challenges I simply wanted out. But, pains I tried to avoid and toiled with eventually became fertile ground for personal development and growth. The beautiful thing about a 'loss' is, especially for those of you who despise losing, it provides an imperfect image of what you *can* correct *and perfect*. Your 'losses' contain hidden and valuable information that is ready for you to learn from, you have the courage to re-encounter them with a fresh, renewed mindset. Be honest, open, and transparent with yourself. Be prepared to investigate your prior losses and victories with these four questions:

1. What did I expect?

2. What happened?

3. What went well/why?

4. What can I improve on from this?

You can and will be victorious. I heard it like this, "Tough times don't last but tough people do." Keep close to heart that when you praise, it is a reminder of what is right. Cutting loose may not mean cutting your losses and counting your losses does not mean you have to quantify your losses as such at all. As a matter of fact, once the Master Surgeon has put his hands into your situation—past, present, or future. Consider this, losses are not only no longer losses, but they are no longer solely yours. You can rest in the victory of Christ Jesus while you calculate your next moves. Go ahead Victor. Fight the good fight, cut loose, and seize your victories.

Power Moves

- Take inventory. Gift yourself a peaceful space and time to thoroughly assess the circumstance(s) you have encountered.

- Ask. Wrestle with yourself through the tough questions of what went right and not quite so right.

- Act. Fear is strengthened by inaction. Act, even if you take mini, or baby steps.

CHAPTER 13

Theresa Noach

Upon discovering the effects of early childhood trauma in her life, Theresa took up the mantle to become a healer by starting within herself. A talented artist born and raised in Florida with passion for music and dance, Theresa decided to change her family's legacy and create a new future for herself and others with the gifts she feels God has given her.

Fear and shame kept Theresa from discovering her self-worth during most of her youth. Determined to let go of every hindering belief system that held her back, Theresa began challenging her core values and theology. The artist describes "falling apart" as a vital part of her initial healing process.

In her upcoming record album, she shares original music composed during this painful and liberating journey to becoming a BOLD woman who is relentlessly living her true purpose. In between directing the children's program, cooking food for the homeless, and planning a worship set, Theresa prioritized her family first. While homeschooling her two daughters for eight years, she taught herself just enough piano, and guitar to write lullabies in which to sing them to sleep.

Theresa describes her husband Joe as a "constant" and "unmovable" support for her evolving ministry and career. They have been married for fifteen years and talk very openly about the ups and downs of marriage and raising a family in the age of technology. "It takes a very secure person to be married to a woman like me" Theresa shares.

"God knew what He was doing when He put us together". Her first book *Un-Raveled* will be ready for a Fall, 2021 release.

Theresa became the Executive Director of Daughters of Naomi, Inc. in 2017 and is currently working to re-launch a residential program for women who are also searching to find wholeness.

The Valiant Principle
Release, Refocus, Relax

Theresa Noach
Singer, Songwriter, Speaker

> *"If I have the gift of prophecy and can fathom all mysteries and all knowledge, and if I have a faith that can move mountains, but have not love, I am nothing."*
>
> **1 Corinthians 13:2**

A pastor I once studied under said, "It is better to choose one thing to put your energy into so that you can do that one thing very well." In some ways I have found this to be true and yet on other occasions this philosophy just does not seem applicable. In my opinion there is no one formula for success, seeing as how there are many types of thinkers and many ways to accomplish a goal based on your personality, body, lifestyle, and other metrics. Everyone has a set of intrinsic strengths and limitations. Trying to understand them is half the battle up this mountain of bold success in life.

Recognize and avoid burnout

It is not always what you do, but how you do it that matters most. Productivity should not wipe you out physically, mentally, or emotionally. Understanding toxic stress as opposed to normal stress is important when making healthy assessments about your time management. Sometimes people have a habit of leaving the starting line in a sprint when they should really be doing a fast walk or slow jog. If you start the race too quickly and begin to feel yourself wearing out, you can learn how to detect this before it is too late to re-calibrate your speed. "The past leaves clues", Dr. Larthenia Howard said to me on one of my first meetings with her. When has your body told you that you were in burn out, but you did not heed the warnings? How did that effect your overall productivity? Sometimes people tend to start over caffeinating to keep up with their own demands. In that case, their insensitivity to what they really need leads them to a dead end of fatigue and a weakened immune system at the very least. For many over achievers this type of push, push, push, leads to major health issues later in life. Unfortunately, this can cause a dream or career to be terminated prematurely.

Reasoning with these limitations is beneficial. Learn to see them as healthy boundaries and a means for considering your life with developed gratitude. For example, one might say that being a "stay at home" mother restricts my ability to pursue a music career or publish my writings. To some capacity this would be an appropriate observation if you were to compare my limitations to that of another person who is not married with children. Now, when you add in other factors such as efficacy, and skill, you might find that as a forty-two-year young woman with three children and a husband, I have developed the ability to manage many more tasks at one time than I did at the age of twenty-five and before starting a family. The key here is if you are going to compare, you must do so with apples to apples and oranges to oranges. I have also heard it said, "Do not compare yourself to someone else". I would say, learn how to measure the differences in a constructive manner.

Comparison allows us to see where we have different faculties and unique ways to offer our skill set to the world and even monetize them. When you examine your mistakes as an opportunity to thrive and expand, failure becomes the torch that keeps burning bright through uncertain times. When you remember that failure in the past does not mean defeat, you can push yourself beyond your weaknesses and perceived limits. As an athlete trains, they will push their bodies beyond that which is comfortable and sometimes in seemingly impossible capacities. However, this push is usually done in a methodical and controlled manner, not in a reactive manner. The key is to give yourself space to stretch and become uncomfortable wherever you are in the process of personal growth.

A time to release

Give yourself the freedom to push beyond yesterday's limitations. I have learned that if I take on the mindset that my Divine Creator allows seasons in my life that seem to extend beyond my comfort zone, then I can maintain an open heart. Your heart must stay open to new possibilities that come from within the challenges of life. Frequently these opportunities look like curveballs. Financial losses, family death, tragedy, and sickness can feel like the end of you when really, they are just the beginning. I find that when I lean into the voice of God, I learn how to see the chance for new beginnings beyond all the sorrow of disappointment.

Sometimes opportunities are forced downtime. If you face tragedy, or sickness and the circumstances seem to put a stop to your dreams and goals, you must learn to see this as a good time to release, refocus and relax. This was the case for me and my family in the summer of 2017. A category five hurricane encroached upon the coast of Florida where Joe and I owned our first home. We moved there in 2014 convinced that this was a steppingstone purchase towards our goal of owning real estate and having rental properties. I was convinced that God gave us a 3–5-year window in which we were to prepare to move again into something bigger that best suited our growing family's needs. Previously we rented a spacious home in a beautiful, gated community with all the amenities that made living there so great. I homeschooled my little girls and spent many days strolling the neighborhood, splashing in the pool, and pushing the girls on the swings. I would have loved to buy our first home in that community, but we wanted to be wise and intentional about our first investment property. We sought a home that would make a suitable rental for a small family, something that would be manageable to us as first time Landlords.

Just outside this gated community was a quaint and wooded town called Lakewood Park. Our new little home quickly became a trophy of success for Joe and me. Within the first few months of moving, our family decided it was time to expand. Though we thought we were done having children, God had different plans. One morning I was overcome with the strongest desire to have another baby! This was not just any old baby fever moment. I was long past those days. This was strangely powerful. I began to ask God if this was from Him, and if so, did He see that we just moved into a smaller house and downsized our entire life? Did He see that I enrolled into a fitness competition and that we decided to get a big dog? We were headed completely away from the idea of having any more children. With every question, the urge became more intense. So, I surrendered and said, "Okay Lord, if this is your will, then you obviously have to get Joe on the same page". Joe and I had discussed a third child many times before moving away from the idea completely.

Joe agreed to giving it a try—if you know what I mean, and that is all she wrote. We conceived our third child, Joseph, born in

August of 2015. During those days, I would strap my son to my chest and do my usual homeschool lessons, children's church planning, and worship team practices. I cooked, cleaned, and got cozy in our new home. As I sought God in prayer, I began to pray for expansion. Without fully understanding why I was praying this, I continued to ask for it. One day I heard in my spirit, "Have you made room for expansion?" I began looking around our small house and thinking about how yet again, I needed to clean out the closets and drawers and get organized in preparation of greater things that were on the horizon. Before too long, we approached the third year of living in our new home and our baby was coming up on his one-year birthday. The voice of God seemed to get stronger within my heart, "Are you ready for expansion?", "Make room."

So, I started looking beyond the natural for what may still be hindering my own personal ability to expand from within. I asked Holy Spirit to reveal anything in my life, and in my heart that hinders growth and my capacity to be filled to a greater measure of God's love. I urged my husband in that we needed to start looking for the next house to buy. We were quickly outgrowing this one with our one-hundred-pound lab and three children. The timing seemed so off. My husbands' career in the car business was on pins and needles and becoming increasingly more stressful for him. The sales were declining but the workload was becoming more oppressive. Joe did not want to think about moving at a time like this. He prayed anyway. Despite how he felt, he looked to God to guide him. Soon, he agreed to start looking for another property. We did not know how we were going to make this shift and what exactly we were supposed to do to prepare. I began talking to an agent about buying but soon realized that this was going to be harder than I had expected. We would have to rent our house to an eligible tenant who was willing to wait for us to move out. Upon finding this applicant, we would have to get them to sign a lease and pay up front for our home to get a lender to off-set that mortgage which would free up the funds we need to finance the next home. This just seemed to get even more complicated with every turn. Even if we found a tenant and moved out, where would we go? How could we afford to rent something else, pay for storage, pack, move, and get this house ready to be rented? How could I physically do all that and maintain everything else? I could not.

By this time hurricane season was upon us and the flooding had already become an issue on our block. We had been through plenty of these storms in the past and was ready for this one. We stocked up on supplies and shuttered the windows, but the waters outside kept rising towards our property line. Hurricane Irma had not even made it on land and was expected to make a connection with our coast the following day. The worst was yet to come. We were very particular to purchase a home that was not in a flood zone, so flooding was not on our radar! Suddenly, water began to come in through the pipes in our bathrooms and we knew we needed to evacuate. A close friend of ours had already invited us to stay with them and fortunately drove a big enough truck that he was able to drive onto our street which had vanished beneath almost two feet of water. We left our house that day with a few suitcases that included important documents, and our dog. We never went back.

Over the next week, we would find out that almost all our belongings were waterlogged and almost every wall in our house was going to have to be gutted. A team of volunteers showed up to assist us in packing everything that could be packed and loaded onto a trailer. For the next two months we lived in one large room in our dear friends' home as we waited minute by minute for God to provide wisdom and resources to make the next step. We cried, fought, and nearly threw in the towel. One thing after another went awfully wrong and somehow still perfectly right. The hardest thing to do was relax, release, and refocus. Such is life.

If you wait for the right time to take care of the things that are in the way, life will do it for you, and it may not feel like a joy ride. It is not unusual for a hurricane to have many sub cells or tornados within them—leaving its victim to feel slammed repeatedly. That is what it felt like for us. Shortly after we found a place to rent, Joe lost his job. No sooner than he lost his job, God provided a new opportunity. Two weeks before the Christmas holiday, the ceiling in the apartment we were renting flooded and had to be completely removed. Somehow through it all, Gods plans for us remained. We bought our second home January 2018 just after finishing the renovations on our first property and finding a tenant to occupy it.

The years to come did not get easier. I would have to write an entire manuscript on the disastrous events that continued to befall us even after we arrived at this new promised land. What I can tell you is that I had to learn how to live in a place of peace and it took time and trials to develop that ability. I am not sure if there was any way to avoid any of these tragic events. It seems as if God has required us to pass through this fire, but we always know He is with us. Other times, we have paid dearly in time and resources for not listening to the re-routing of God and changing our course when we sensed it was time to do so.

A time to refocus

If you set out with a goal or a plan and life show you that you are headed in the wrong direction, are you willing to put your pride down and change directions? This is God's way of re-routing your GPS system. We often miss these "U-Turn" moments for fear of letting others down. Once you have shared your detailed visions with friends and families, and hosted the Vision Board Party, it's hard to admit you went the wrong way. However, you must be willing to stand in your sacred space no matter what direction the Creator calls you to go. When life presents opportunities to reset, and you can bet it will, you must be sensitive to that redirection. In these seasons, I found it most humbling to have to accept help from others. I needed help with the clean-up. We needed somewhere to live, and even financial support.

You must allow the caring love of others to lift you up, strengthen you, and care for you when you are weak. So often a person with tenacity and drive also struggles with the antagonistic traits of individualism. While these attributes have the tendency to carry tremendous beauty and strength, they also can present a problem when gone unchecked. These behavioral patterns are only beneficial when you are balanced and know who you are as a divine being with infinite potential. Busyness is often a sign that you have not learned to trust others and to release some of your tasks to capable hands. In these moments, you will not allow others an opportunity to fail—just as they do not allow themselves to fail. Many times, you will hold on to goals from fear of failure even though life you the goal was wrong to begin with. If you are in anyway like me, you likely will not delegate jobs that are holding you back from obtaining your goals because you cannot stand the idea of the task not being completed to your standard. However, if you allow others in your life to fail and or succeed, you will find that the burden of having to do things by yourself will become lighter. You can learn to flow in the imperfectly perfect energy for this season of your life. Then it is made obvious that even the unexpected so-called failures are gifts from heaven—sent to propel you in the direction you were created to go. Just when I thought I could not handle any more pressure or unexpected difficulties, more came. I did not crumble. I thought I might. However, I stood on the unfailing love of God and His word.

> "We are hard pressed on every side, but not crushed; perplexed, but not in despair; 9 persecuted, but not abandoned; struck down, but not destroyed. 10 We always carry around in our body the death of Jesus, so that the life of Jesus may also be revealed in our body."
>
> **2 Corinthians 4:8-10**

Whatever story is active within your subconscious about who you are to yourself, to God, and to others is going to continually try to balance itself within your daily activities. For example, if internally you do not honestly believe that you can accomplish that goal, and you begin to actualize that thing or you begin to succeed at your micro goals, subconsciously you will take on activities that do not align with that goal. Your subconscious will bring you back into balance with the concept that you will not accomplish your objective. This theory can seem very discouraging, but the more you understand and embrace it, the more you can allow yourself to be rewired by beliefs that align with your true intention and purpose in life. Busyness is a great indicator that your subconscious lower self has taken over and the higher self has lost control of the fight forward. You can literally do this to yourself. The part of you that does not agree with your intention is the portion of yourself that does not agree with what Creator has fashioned you to be and do. These occurrences that are burning you out are likely the fruit of a narrative that is planted like a seed subconsciously in your mind. Realizing this will empower and propel you to seek the support and coaching you need to reprogram your internal processes.

Caroline Leaf is an author and speaker who has many publications on this topic. The Bible says to *be transformed by the renewing of your mind*. Quantum physicist and neuroscientist have explained these events in scientific terms as more and more evidence come to light. Your life truly can be changed when your thoughts are interchanged. Thoughts create matter and that matter potentially becomes your environments, relationships, careers, and goals. A busy life and a busy mind are not conducive to a productive and satisfying existence. A busy life produces stress. A productive life accomplishes a feeling of satisfaction. A stressful life produces sickness, whereas a satisfying life produces health.

A recent book that I read by Jeffrey Rediger, M.D., "Cured", describes one man's beautiful journey into the research of spontaneous remission. Each member of the case study had one thing in common and that was that they were all given a terminal medical prognosis and extraordinarily little time to live. Each of them, ten years later or more, were thriving and living their best lives. In many of the cases the clients who had gotten sick also had toxically stressful lives in common. Some of them were in unhealthy relationships while others were overworked in jobs that they were not the least bit happy with, or in partnerships that were not satisfying. When faced with their own mortality and physical limitations, they began to see every minute of life as more valuable than before. They began to cherish life and learned to live from a place of acceptance which led to peace. For many of them, they had to release things they had been holding on to. They had to allow their sickness to reset their lives so they could at least live what they had left with meaning. That deep change, that reset in their soul caused their lives to be extended beyond scientific projection, and most of them reported feeling a sense of fulfilling their lives work.

For the *dreamer*, a detailed futuristic perspective is the norm. However, these individuals are commonly the ones who struggle to set realistic goals and muster up the determination to make their dreams a reality. For the *tasker*, a To Do List and the lack of discipline is not the problem. It is having to dream and design a road map that for them seems impossible. The dreamer will have to practice daily efforts of finishing small tasks and appreciating their accomplishments as they determine to get more organized and routine. The tasker will have to develop the art of daydreaming, and relaxing. I believe most people tend to fall in one category or the other. You have probably heard the terms "Right and Left brained". Those are the two types of people I am talking about here. One side of the brain tends to be more dominant. Finding out which one you fit into will help your strengths and weaknesses differently and hopefully you can appreciate them more. Find partners with the skill sets you do not have and practice developing in the areas you need growth. In some cases, it pays to hire the person who thrives where you do not. If you do not have the budget for that, then learn to be resourceful and make helpful connections.

A mantra I live by is, "Help others get what they need, and you will always have what you need." Go into new relationships with something to contribute and soon you will be linked with others who also have something you need. It is especially important to determine if your relationships and partnerships are conducive for moving you closer to your desired outcome. A good question to ask yourself is whether your daily activities and habits are compounding to bring you closer to your objective. Are there responsibilities that you can delegate? Take some time evaluate where your energy is going and hit the reset button whenever necessary. That sounds so simple, but it can be difficult especially if you are committed to something.

Integrity is so important to your future, and you cannot afford to commit to activities that you may have to back out of. Reliability and dependability are hard qualities to find sometimes. You must ask yourself if you are reliable and dependable. If not, then why would life give you anything more than you earned? If hitting the reset button means breaking a commitment, I would suggest you be true to what you are called to do but do it with caution so that the next time you commit, you truly hesitate and consider how this will align with your path. Aiming to be balanced spiritually, emotionally, and physically will help to keep you on track.

Maybe you are in the prime of your life feeling strong, healthy, and full of vitality. Some of you may be feeling an urgency as if you are coming to the end of your prime and you have deadlines on the things that you know you want to do in this life. Regardless of where you are, can you think of a time when your body decided to put you in a reset mode? Maybe a breakup, an injury, divorce, or even a loved one's death caused you to experience a season of depression where you experienced a reset. If you have not taken the time to sit down and to think about what life wanted to communicate with you during that time, perhaps now is a better time than ever. Create space. Sometimes this process starts on the outside first and other occasions, creating space happens from within—and then our exterior lives align with that. Then there is the simultaneous experience of physically creating space. That is while you are organizing your shelves your closets and your files, you are also experiencing a type of spiritual and emotional purge. Each season of growth in my life has been marked by a notable time of purging. Whether or not I initiate the purging, it always seems to happen right before a launching season into the next phase of God's intentions for myself, marriage, and our family.

A time to relax

Sometimes the thought of relaxing and doing something good or fun for yourself seems unimportant. Even if your career is something you are passionate about and you get rejuvenated by completely immersing yourself in your work, a time of changing the scenery and receiving a bit of pampering goes along way.

I tend to be very driven, so relaxing has become something I do very intentionally. Whether I am submerging myself in projects around the house and with the kids or working on content for my professional platforms and websites, I love what I do. I get charged doing the things I am passionate about, but I also am still only human and get fatigued. Years ago, this overwork led to emotional and mental break downs that negatively affected my relationships and peace. By "break downs" I mean, snapping, getting rude, yelling at the kids, rejecting my husband, or getting upset with myself. Other times a "break down" would mean "set back". I would experience a setback in my momentum, nutrition, and healthy habits. Everything changed for the better when I learned to know my body's cues. I started listening to God AND my God given intuition. I see intuition as more of a God given attribute that all human beings have, truly the sixth sense.

You can learn to listen to this physical prompting to change. Feelings of irritability, weariness, and frustration are indicators that you have gone off balance with your work/pleasure ratios. You may have to reschedule meetings or re-arrange time to suit your actual needs. Take a nap, go for a walk, listen to music, meditate/pray, call a friend—these are all ways you can get re-calibrated and refreshed.

I am a bit spoiled by the coast of Florida and can take a beach day any given time. Finding a place to connect with nature can be a fabulous way to refresh your body and your spirit. Taking a walk in the park, turning off the phone calls, putting in earbuds and listening to some classical music or something slow always helps to re-calibrate my energy. Depending on the number of projects I am juggling, it may take me longer to get into a place of serenity, so I must allow myself the time and space to fully unwind. I have found that many people struggle to allow themselves to be still.

Recently my husband started using an app to assist him in this area. The app starts by reminding him a few times a day to take a one-minute pause. During that pause, he listens to the sound of ambient tunes and guided meditation. The app turns the minute into two minutes, and then to five, and eventually to ten. The goal is to help the individual improve their ability to calm their mind and their heart, and to train themselves in becoming still.

For many overachievers, this is difficult to do. Notice I said "over "achievers. Overachievers are not necessarily balanced or achieving much of anything valuable. Often overachievers have an inner child that is still trying to win the approval of mom, dad, and others. This is one of the reasons why it is hard for an overachiever to be still. Being still means you must begin to wrestle with the thoughts that fuel your activity. In the moments of stillness, the deeper emotions and thoughts begin to surface. That is honestly a wonderful thing, but it is also when a person may feel uncomfortable with racing thoughts.

Most people would rather be busy than face the wounded inner child. Many times, achievement is the escape of a persons unhealed soul. To be still would require them to settle into their imperfections. For me, that is where faith in God comes into play. The Bible says that God glories in my weakness. Believing that helps me to embrace my flaws or the trauma of the past. By "embrace" I do not mean "keep", I mean "accept and release".

Giving yourself an opportunity to refresh will often create a pathway for you to release toxic emotions attached to old memories. With a little help and guidance, you can begin to rewire your brain with gratitude. When you start to express gratitude for the way you have come through all the difficulties of life, you can begin to appreciate the lessons your difficulties have brought you. You may realize that some of the things you thought of as being parts of success, in fact were just ways you were overcompensating. In the end, when you face these toxic emotions that you have spent a lifetime avoiding, you can let go of the activities in your lives that honestly serve no purpose in your destiny.

When you are connected to Creator, and flowing in Holy Spirit through God's Son, I believe your body will cue you correctly. Your body's signals are your thermostat for life. These signals tell you when to adjust things to bring your *being* into homeostasis. Sometimes life requires that you sprint, but most of the time it is best to learn a steady pace by which to aim for your goals. Slow and steady truly does win—most of the time! There is no format to copy and paste from one successful person to the next. It takes time and patience to learn the system that works best for you.

Relax. Take a break. Breathe. It all works out in the end if you stay the course.

power moves

- Stay in your lane. It is where you will run your best race.

- Pace yourself. Life is big and has bumps in the road.

- Allow yourself the freedom to push pass yesterday's limitations.

CHAPTER 14

Kay Bodude, RN, BSN

Kay Bodude has been married to Ebenezer Bodude for 22 years as of March 2021. She is the mother of seven aspiring young adults: Terrail, Nathean, Caymen, Kaylynn Philip, Emily, Elana, and Elexis. When Kay was growing up in Kansas City, Missouri with nine of her fourteen siblings and living in a three-bedroom house, she never expected to one day be the co-Owner of a multi-million-dollar group home empire: an author, or a mentor of over 100 entrepreneurs.

Kay moved from Mississippi when she was only a toddler. Her parents, who were sharecroppers, wanted a better life for their children. Deciding early on at the age of eight that she liked helping people, she set her mind on becoming a nurse. During her first job at age 13 as a candy striper (volunteer), she knew healthcare was her passion. Her focus turned towards behavioral health when her older sister was diagnosed with Schizophrenia and Bipolar Disorder.

Kay would go on to not only achieve her dreams of becoming a Registered Nurse, practicing in a clinical capacity for over 25 years, but she discovered she had a knack for business and became what she proclaimed as a business catalyst. Being a "catalyst", Kay assists other entrepreneurs to find and reach their life purpose in business. Kay has traveled to several different countries in the past few years, in which she feels meeting and socializing with people from different backgrounds has catapulted her into "Living her best Authentic Life".

Tell the Truth, Shame the Devil

Live Your Best Authentic Life...An Entrepreneur's Perspective

Kay Bodude, RN, BSN
Best Care Behavioral Homes, Co-owner

> *"Success is to be measured not so much by the position that one has reached in life as by the obstacles which he has overcome while trying to succeed."*
>
> **Booker T. Washington, American educator**

How many of you would be living a totally different life if you were FREE within yourselves? Some of you are in relationships you should not be in, have debt that is not working for you, in positions/careers you really do not want. Many of you are where you are in life because if you admit it, you were playing it safe, or ignoring your authentic self. Stay with me here. I have found myself in the same place repeatedly. If you are anything like many people I know, including myself, you have probably compared yourself to family, friends, co-workers, and people you have no meaningful relationship to at all. For some, comparison is a way to justify a comfort zone or to point fingers because at least you are better off than that person over there. Most people never reach their full potential or purpose in life. They become victim to the comparison kill, play small, get trapped by web of opinions of others, or simply settle for the comfort familiarity. It is a common story for the average person to believe many different reasons why the comfort zone is a safe place. To break this pattern, you must be willing to change. To rise above average requires you to move beyond circles of influence that stifle growth. Until you make this move, you will not experience what it means to truly be free.

In retrospect, there were many times when I was not claiming my FREE-ness. I am a mother of seven who gave birth to my first child at 17 years old. Most of my older sisters and some of their friends had their first child around the age of seventeen. I took out high student loans to complete college, instead of working and paying as I moved along. I continued to go to church not because I desired to, but because it was what I was expected to do on Sundays. Are you getting the picture? Your environment molds and conditions you to stay within an imaginary box. It never dawned on me that there were options for me to not have children or even not to continue having children. If I knew I had options, there most likely would not have been a number 2, 3, 4, 5, 6, or 7. Do not misunderstand me. I love my children. My point is I was living the life my environment, society, family, friends, and coworkers had set the tone for me to follow.

> *"Whatever we believe about ourselves and our ability comes true for us."*
>
> **Susan L. Taylor, American editor**

A proclamation to be free

I moved to Arizona as a proclamation of wanting to be FREE (Finally Reaching Exponential Expectations). In Scripture, 3 John 2 states, *"Beloved, I wished above all things thou may prosper and be in health, even as thy soul prospers."* Your family and those in your inner circle may not agree on the way you live your life when you decide to be FREE, but you know what is best for you when you tap into the inner voice, that stirring inside of you that nudges you in a particular direction. For me, the zone of truth feels as a river of renewed energy flows through my veins. When I walk in my truth, all pressures of life decisions appear lifted from my shoulders. Authenticity is freeing. You will know it when your spirit soars like a butterfly, light and effortless on your flight of life.

How many of you believe you have a purpose in life or know there is something special you are supposed to accomplish? Part of your purpose may be to become a well-known author, businessperson, to start a bakery, travel to parts of the world as a missionary, help undeveloped countries bring water to towns without indoor plumbing, be the best mom or dad you can be, or be the first in your family to go to college or become a millionaire. How do you know this? Do you ever get an overwhelming feeling about certain things you cannot shake, turn-off, or easily forget? This thing stirs you up inside, it wakes you up at night, it almost feels like anxiety—the feeling of a ball of positive energy demanding to be pushed out into the atmosphere. God puts this feeling inside of you so you can push forth to the purpose of life he destined for you. It is your choice to travel this journey or sit back and allow life to pass you up as you watch other people live their purpose.

Have you ever wondered "When will it be my time to shine?" Well, here is the real deal—wondering will get you nowhere.

When you are determined, you will make a way, or find a way to not only be invited to the table, but build a table. To make a path for yourself, you must set specific, realistic, and time limited goals. These three items are very important to keep you on track because goal setting is only the beginning. When you know where you are trying to go and goals are set, you then must work through the process of meeting your goals. Use a planner like the *Kay Bodude's Goal Setting Planner* to keep track of your progress. It only takes the faith of a mustard seed to move mountains. And it only takes direction to keep moving forward.

Why you should not "Fake it until you make it"

In my experience with a home business, I was encouraged by an advising leadership team to fake it until I could make it. There was so much I did not know and a lot I did not know I did not know. It was certainly a growth experience. Good and bad examples were all around me at the time. I cringe now just thinking about many of the decisions I was presented with in the process of trying to build something from scratch for which I had little knowledge—especially when it came to the financial aspects of the business. I could see how it would have been easy to go into debt, ruin credit, and be left with excess inventory when trying to market company products to increase income. However, the truth of who I am would not allow me to venture down that route, and several mentors parted ways with me because of the decision.

Honoring who you are is more important than becoming someone you are not, just to appease others. I learned many valuable business and personal skills in those early days of building a business. More importantly, I became comfortable with being pushed outside my comfort zone. I learned how to speak the language of business, how to cold call, market a business, brand, and present my ideas clearly. And the most valuable lesson of all was learning not give up when times get tough. These are lessons I took with me as I developed my own business and life strategies to grow my multimillion-dollar business. Every lesson and life experience helped me to become a master at crafting a space for my own freedom in thoughts and behaviors. Sometimes you simply must recognize why you were put into a situation. Acknowledge what you need to learn from situations. Use uncomfortable circumstances to your advantage and be courageous enough to walk away if the move gets you closer to your purpose.

As the old cliche goes... *Honesty is truly the best policy*. My most successful self and business evolved from a self-honesty policy. Trust yourself, be confident in knowing what you know and take risks. Without this skill, you will never know your capabilities. Know this, just because an idea is not successful, does not mean it is a failure. Learn from the flop, take the good from it, and move to the next venture. For this and many other reasons, diligence is so important. You must be diligent in the ability to easily revamp or move when you realize something is not engaging as you expected.

#BOYBB

How many times has someone gotten you to act out of your normal character? If you are honest, you would be quick to raise your hand. I have only met one person with the patience of Job. She was the Nurse Dean at MidAmerica Nazarene University where I completed my Bachelor's in Nursing. This professor would be so calm even in the tensest moments. Her calm would calm your spirit. Why mention this? Well because while thinking of all the times I could have, maybe should have, and did lose my cool, I stumbled upon a new way of thinking. The acronym #BOYBB transformed my life—literally. I know this may sound simple, but this message was so clear to me when I started my career as an entrepreneur. The idea is simply this—Be On Your Best Behavior. The old folks would say "It is easier to catch a fly with honey than vinegar". Meaning. a little kindness can go a long way. Here are a few ways I found the concept of #BOYBB to be helpful, particularly in my business. Hopefully one or more will resonate with you as well.

Be respectful. Time is Money. As part of the #BOYBB mantra, I strive to always be respectful of people's time. This includes arriving early to navigate surprises. I find myself repeating, "Time is money". No matter what you say or do, you can never reclaim lost or misused time. Along with the respect of time is the respect of boundaries and expertise. Many times, entrepreneurs want information but are not willing to invest. To effectively grow your business, you need proper guidance and mentorship. The money and time it takes to do this is to be respected. To effectively grow your business obtaining guidance and mentorship is a natural progression and money and time investments demand respect.

Be diligent. I remember when our team was trying to get our first group home started—we faced so much opposition. It seemed liked there was one issue after another. Insurance companies tried to low-ball us on the reimbursement amount, county officials lost paperwork, or they processed paperwork so slow that 30 days would pass before getting a signature. Sometimes we were flat out ignored over the phone, email, or during in person visits to the office. I could have lost my cool and acted out of character. However, I chose to remain focused on the goal. Diligence requires focus. There were many challenges my business partners, management team, and I faced when trying to reach our annual goals of passing the million-dollar mark for Best Care Home Services—but we stayed the course. The goal was and remains bigger than our individual agendas. Again, this focus demands diligence, or for each of us to keep our eyes on the prize.

Be patient. I cannot recount the number of opportunities presented that could have pressed me into quick decision making. While building a business, I encountered so many different people with different ideas and competing agendas. Frustration visited my door several times, but I held my peace and allowed my mentor, Heavenly Father, to fight my battles. I envisioned Him appearing in those meeting rooms while the committees were discussing Best Care. I could see Him changing hearts and minds for our good. I was constantly reminded of the big picture. I had to ask myself, "Do you want the instant gratification of giving people a piece of your mind? Or do you want to continue moving forward to build a legacy and generational wealth for your family and friends?" I choose the latter. Patience is truly a virtue.

Be consistent. According to Webster, consistent is "acting or done in the same way overtime, especially so as to be fair or accurate." This concept is important in how you do business because it determines what customers grow to expect from your services. Consistency plays a huge role in your reputation. Imagine if you depended on my company's transportation route to transport you to your routine weekly appointments. If we arrived at 9:00 am this Monday, 8:30 am next Monday, and then showed up at 9:15 am the following week...what a mess? You get the picture. Many of the important life lessons you learned as a child are no different than what you should observe as a business owner. Strive to, "Do unto others as you would have them do unto you".

Be prepared. The difference between the "wrong" time and the "right" time is your preparation. In the book of Matthew 24, the Bible reminds us to "always be ready". You never know when your preparation may equate to a new contract, speaking engagement, or meeting someone who is influential in elevating to you to the next step on your journey. Sometimes I feel my team and I are such perfectionists. We tend to overdo things. But, in those times when we were overprepared, we seized major opportunities.

Be self-motivated. Self-motivation can be described as the force driving you to do things—the force driving people to keep going even in the face of setbacks. Self-motivated individuals count so-called failures not as failures, but as opportunities for learning and growth. You must thirst for challenges and be willing to take risks. Most people say find your reason why, but self-motivated individuals live and breathe their reasons why. Most days I have to calm my spirit because I am so motivated about ideas, opportunities, and upcoming events. My motivated spirit can often feel like anxiety—in a good way. So, pause here to ponder, "What am I self-motivated about to the point it makes me anxious—in a good way?"

Be trustworthy. This is simple but profound—say what you mean and mean what you say. Do not be one of those people who talk the talk but does not walk the talk. Your words are your reputation, your brand. Be who you want others to believe you are.

Tell the truth and shame the devil

When you live in your truth and share your authenticity with others, you can hold your head up high. This is where the phrase *"Tell the truth and shame the devil"* derived. While some people can be 100, or fully honest with themselves and others most of the time, a lot of people struggle with authenticity. Masks are as real for adults as they are for a child dressed in a Halloween custom. Imposter syndrome is real as people vacillate between their real self and the self they project to the world. Here is my invitation to you to finally live in your truth and walk in the beauty in which you were created. I invite you to be F.R.E.E. (Finally Reaching Exponential Expectations).

F.R.E.E. in peace. There are so many things in life that will try to keep you from experiencing peace. I am reminded of the things that used to keep me up at night or caused me to be angry with myself. I can admit this now without crying, but at one point in my teenage life, I considered suicide to escape misery. It is unfortunate but so many teenagers are made to feel or believe they are inadequate. Equally disheartening is the number of adults who feel this way too. The evil of comparison, social media, the opinions of others, and messages we receive from those around us have a way of injecting self-doubt. You may question your self-worth or value. Low self-esteem is prevalent, and depression is at an all-time high. However, the good news is this: you were created with a purpose and for a purpose.

F.R.E.E. in hope. When I think about standing in truth, I realize family and those you love sometimes inflicts hurt the most. Sometimes this is intentional but most often I believe it is unintentional. Words matter, and they especially matter most when delivered by those you love the most. Remember this, "Weeping may endure for the night, but Joy comes in the morning." What that means is, if you can hold on for a little while longer, life is going to get better.

F.R.E.E. is strength. I implore you to come to terms with life circumstances on your life journey. Find courage. Find strength. Scream from the housetop, seek therapy, or journal to your heart is content. Find your center and do whatever it takes to live in your truth day by day. Release the lies you may have told yourself about yourself. Or maybe you need to release the lies others have told you about you that—those you consciously or unconsciously believe. Either way, if they are not serving you well, release them. Conquer your journey and walk in the essence of who you are created to be in the here and now.

What does it mean to be F.R.E.E.?

F - Finally

R - Reaching

E - Exponential "becoming more and more rapidly"

E - Expectation "a belief someone will or should achieve something"

Power Moves

- Claim your Free-ness to finally reach exponential expectations.

- Set specific, realistic, and time limited goals.

- Trust yourself, be confident in knowing what you know and take risks.

CHAPTER 15

Christina Rampersad

With over 30 years of international entrepreneurial, human development, leadership, and outreach experience, Christina Rampersad is known for her ability to educate, empower and inspire others to live a phenomenal life of purpose, passion, and resilience. Christina is a Human Development CEO, Transformation Strategist, Resilience Expert, Faith Leader, Author, and Board Certified Coach.

As the creator of the Success Beyond the Brink System, Christina has globally impacted lives with her proven strategies to eliminate barriers, create clarity, build confidence, and increase momentum. Christina has great mastery in business and a wealth of wisdom to share. However, it has been her life mastery lessons, learning how to persevere despite emotional, physical, and mental trauma, while trusting God for something greater, that provides her the tremendous ability to authentically serve others.

As the Founder of Success Beyond the Brink™ International, V.O.I.C.E. Community Development Corporation and Shekinah Outreach International, Christina has been blessed to share her message of faith, perseverance, and empowerment on international stages, radio, as well as television, including TBN. In addition, she has co-authored *Ushering in the Apostolic Anointing* with her husband, Robin Rampersad. Her new writings *Success Beyond the Brink*™ and *Understanding Prophetic Ministry* are scheduled to soon be released.

Christina's mission is to eradicate suffering and pain worldwide while cultivating a culture of hope, love, and purpose. She has always lived by her life motto "Persistence Overcome Resistance" and encourages people to believe that "The Future is Brighter Than the Present." Christina loves spending time by the ocean, experiencing new adventures, and creating lasting memories. She is passionate about seeing others live on purpose and fully alive. She is grateful for the privilege of life and sharing it with her husband, Robin, and son, Tristyn. She's their biggest fan! In addition, Christina has been gifted with the opportunity to provide fulltime care for her mom.

Stand Still

Persevere When it Matters

Christina Rampersad
Success Beyond the Brink™, Founder

> *"You don't make progress by standing on the sidelines, whimpering and complaining. You make progress by implementing ideas."*
>
> **Shirley Chisholm, American politician**

Cultivate stillness

Today, we live in a world where chaos, trauma and hurriedness remain the norm. Having to rise above it and thrive requires not only commitment but discipline. Whether the demand in your relationship, employment or other pressing circumstance is vying for attention, one thing remains certain, a lot of the day is spent multitasking. Globally, this issue of hurriedness can cause overcommitment and overwhelm while operating at accelerated speed. This type of lifestyle can cause significant harm to your health, relationships, and life. Daily, stillness beckons you for the purpose of mastering it. If anyone understands the busyness of life and multiple layers of responsibilities, I do. In addition to running several corporations and contributing life impacting value around the world, I am a wife, homeschooling mom, as well as a full-time caregiver for my mother. There are many days filled with tremendous opportunity for me to persevere when it matters. However, it took a while for me to understand the significance of standing still.

As a courageous go getter, I have always lived from a place of persistence. Since childhood, I press until what I envision manifests. However, because of life's unexpected, I have been gifted with the opportunity to learn flexibility while realizing the magnitude of stillness. Stillness is the state of cultivating calm, minimizing motion, and practicing peace. This state is created by turning your attention away from internal and external distraction while quieting your thoughts and emotions. In this powerful moment, you are open to receive new insight in addition to strategy for everything that you are encountering. If you experience opposition to achieving stillness, please know that you are not alone. In fact, many people battle internal along with external enemies. Internally, the struggle includes anxiety, worry, fear, overcommitment, limiting belief, and self-sabotage. Externally, a demanding relationship, overwhelm of responsibility, lack of time, or hardship tend to pose a challenge. Either way, making space in your life for stillness requires intentionality and commitment.

Maintaining a healthy approach to this belief will prove vital for your overall well-being and success. When you sense opposition attempting to deter you from peace, consider identifying the root of it. Ask yourself powerful questions. What trigger resulted in the current reaction? When was the first time you experienced this distraction? Do your emotions or thoughts connect with a specific person, place, or event? When you notice one of these enemies trying to invade your mind and emotion, choose to stop, become aware, and redirect your attention to the present moment.

Tremendous strength comes from living in the moment. Anxiety is living in the future while worrying about the outcome of a situation before it happens. Regret is living in the past along with attempting to change an existing outcome. Being present to the moment requires deliberate engagement of the brain and heart. When you identify your internal and external enemy, eradicate the barrier to stillness and master being present to the moment, you will stand still. With this stillness you are better equipped to observe what wants to emerge and receive new strength for persevering when it matters.

Change your perspective

To successfully persevere, you must have the fortitude to push beyond any opposition or contrary circumstance to your desired outcome. Once you stand still, adjust your focus, a clear perspective deems the utmost importance. Because of the challenge that life can present, there is a risk of falling prey to a victim mindset. Instead, consider guarding your emotions to avoid feeling like the only one in the world walking through a challenging place without a resolve or cheering squad to get you through. Fortunately, changing your perspective will provide the strength necessary to break through every form of resistance.

While participating in one of Tony Robbin's seminars I gleaned something from him that impacted me significantly. "What if life wasn't happening to you, but happening for you?" What a powerful concept that revolutionized my life forever. Therefore, I say to you, are you choosing the mindset of punishment or progress? Throughout the world, people endure horrible, even heinous things. When others hear my story, they tend to respond with, "Oh my, I could never do it." Instead, with gratitude I respond, "I thank God, because someone else's load could be worse." For a clearer perspective of your burden, contemplate the people who have lost family members, friends, finances, as well as hope during this time of COVID-19. How traumatizing to lose all of this without warning or consent. When you choose to believe that everything is working to progress you towards the fulfillment of your life purpose, adversity is a vehicle to your promotion. At this place of revelation, you will begin to automatically identify your opposition as opportunity for growth.

Whether you are in a mountain top or valley experience, it is vital to maintain an ascended viewpoint. Remember that both are a passageway to the next leg of your journey. Mountains and valleys have different viewpoints; however, both have their advantages. When you are on the mountain you can see farther than in the valley. The higher your altitude the clearer the air. If you ascend above the clouds, you find an unobstructed view. On the mountain you are closer to the sun which serves as a source of illumination in darkness.

Climbing the heights of a mountain mandates the need for more strength to climb. Journeying through the valley provides preparation, contemplation, and inspiration. When you perceive the valley correctly, you acquire the resources, strength, and direction to ascend the mountain. Life does not consist of continual mountain top experiences. Eventually, you go back down to the valley to prepare for the next mountain top experience.

Relocating from the mountain to the valley and vice versa requires movement. This transition brings transformation which results in growth. If you are not growing, you are dying. Therefore, every situation in life provides an opportunity to ultimately become perfected for what lies ahead. Therefore, I invite you to evaluate your present circumstance, explore your lesson, embrace personal development, including master your energy for the purpose of persevering.

Clarify your vision

A foundational necessity for persevering when it matters requires clarifying your compelling vision. Undoubtedly, this desired outcome anchors you to the future. Despite circumstances, people or resources, your vision invigorates you. Just the thought of it makes you feel fully alive. Passion becomes ignited, deep within you know, "I was born for this". This immerses you in the flow of life or what some call living in the zone. The compelling vision compels you to get up in the morning, stay up late at night, endure adversity, learn new skills, foster mutually benefitting relationships, submit to mentors, seek wisdom, and sacrifice any resource with the intention to manifest your purpose. Without a doubt, compelling vision determines the destination in your GPS of life. When you know the destination, the route becomes an option.

Compelling vision tremendously serves you at the core of your being. Fostered by your personal and professional value system it will lead you to connect with people that are heading in the same direction. Strategically, it will eliminate distraction, giving you laser focus. The books you read, places you go, along with the relationships you develop will point towards your intention. The compelling vision serves as the road guide of your journey.

If you lack clarity of vision, consider setting aside time to contemplate and powerfully articulate it. Creating a visual replication of your desired outcome serves as a powerful anchor. Though it may be futuristic or seem impossible, you have the capability to access it in the present moment. Find a space of inner tranquility, close your eyes pus step into it. Ask yourself, what colors do I see, what sounds do I hear, who else occupies this space with me, how do I feel physically also emotionally? This creates an opportunity to experience your sweet spot as if it already exists.

Perhaps, you may not have a compelling vision. However, the fact that you are reading this proves you desire more. However, if there remains uncertainty about your compelling vision, asking yourself some questions will benefit. What will you do all day if money does not require consideration? Whose life will you touch? What service or product will you provide? What part of the nation or world will you live? What could you do every day of your life plus never grow bored, tired, or complacent?

Maybe you already know your compelling vision as well as live it daily. Then, I invite you to consider how you can share your passion with others more effectively. How can you reproduce yourself for future generations? How can you contagiously affect others with courage including zeal? How can you serve more people? How can you expand your market? What can you do to change history from today?

Once you answer these questions you will find yourself experiencing the clarity besides calm necessary to strategize and take the next steps in perseverance.

Master your mindset

Mastering your mindset is key in knowing how to stand still and persevere when it matters. Mindset directly impacts your beliefs with corresponding actions. To successfully plow through resistance, it is imperative to extend self-love. Undoubtedly, giving grace and compassion to yourself while understanding you are not your circumstance makes a difference. Walking in forgiveness towards yourself as well as others provides freedom. Letting go of the past for the purpose of moving forward allows you to press into the future uninhibited. As a tremendous force for good, you can overcome anything. The courage to move beyond rejection, disappointment—including someone else's opinion, creates an inner determination that screams "I will not be stopped". The inner giant arises causing you to feel strengthened in addition to resolved. Together this provides the focus necessary to hit bullseye as you target objectives and bulldoze barriers to your success.

Rejection, along with fear, gives way as confidence arises to take control of planning. Bouncing back with the mindset of resilience enables you to persevere. Resilience means to the ability to recover from setback, disappointment, or delay. Walking in mindset mastery will make the flow of innovation available to you for problem solving while pioneering new direction. A tremendous example that embodies mindset mastery is Walt Disney. Known for enduring rejection, disappointment, lack of support and false accusation, he succeeded despite opposition because of his compelling future together with mindset mastery. As a result of Disney's tenacious propensity to stand still and persevere when it matters, the world continues to experience his vision today.

Persevere when it matters

Practicing stillness, cultivating perspective, clarifying vision, and mastering your mindset position you for success on the journey of persevering when it matters. These steps equip you to forge forward beyond any opposition. In addition, perseverance also requires tenacity as well as resilience. These are skills cultivated in moments of intense challenge. Embracing circumstances enable you to accept the present while planning the future. This does not constitute giving up or forfeiting the expectation. Often battling through conflict expends so much energy while trying to escape a situation that the easy exit goes unnoticed. For example, my mother, a paralyzed stroke survivor requires full time care. For almost eight years, I struggled to find help, frustrated that no one appeared do the job. One day, I surrendered. With trust, I accepted the situation knowing I needed to find a different way of addressing this issue. More importantly, I needed to maintain my peace and contentment even if things never changed.

Acceptance is imperative! Understanding timing is also crucial. Somethings are not delayed or denied. Often, it is just a matter of wait. Ask yourself honestly, Am I prepared for this right now? Is there room in my life for this? Do I have the resources or contacts necessary to accomplish this? Is now the best time for this? When things go contrary to your expectations it is easy to become frustrated or blinded. Sometimes, just knowing the proper timing in life gives the green light to persevere when it matters.

Perseverance requires innovative strategy birthed in the stillness. Having clarity of your desired outcomes will give you the foundation necessary to create and implement strategies to hit the bullseye of purpose. Keep focus, stand strong as you remain resolved to be a victor, not a victim. By engaging your expectations, you will create the healthy environment necessary to persist beyond every distraction, delay or disappointment that may stand in your way.

Stand Still... Persevere when it matters! When does it matter? It matters every time it matters most to you! There are things in life that are trivial and no longer a representation of the dynamic person you have evolved into. Toxic beliefs, relationships in addition to negative conversation, do not warrant your energy or time. Perseverance matters when you know you are born for greatness, you sense a deeper cry for more, or when your present doesn't speak of your desired future. I believe in you! I believe you can stand still and persevere when it matters.

power moves

- Walk in forgiveness towards yourself and others.

- Think this—life is happening for me, not to me.

- Vision determines life's destination and anchors your future. Clarify a compelling vision.

168   The Power of **Bold**

Tammy L. Allen

Tammy Allen is the oldest of seven children, mother to one son, and grandmother of three beautiful princesses. She is the owner of TLA Enterprise of Tampa Bay LLC and earned a bachelor's degree in criminal justice from the University of South Florida. Tammy is a Veteran and Honorably Discharged as Sergeant Allen.

Tammy holds several professional licenses to include Licensed Realtor, Public Claims Adjuster in 8 states: Life, Health, and an Annuity License. The most rewarding part of her real estate career is partnering with local general contractors to build single-family homes in the community. She also holds a Woman-Owned Business Certification and Loan Signing Agent Certification.

Entrepreneurship is part of her DNA. Tammy successfully owned and operated a local childcare center for 18 years. After a breast cancer diagnosis, she decided to resign from the childcare industry. Now, her most rewarding title is SURVIVOR.

Tear It Up to Build It Up

How to Restart and Build Back Better

Tammy L. Allen
TLA Enterprise of Tampa Bay LLC

> *"Never, ever be afraid to make some noise*
> *and get in trouble, necessary trouble."*
>
> **John Lewis, Former U.S. Representative**

After becoming a single parent at an early age, my parents encouraged me to finish high school, go to college, and get a good job. I graduated high school with honors, attended the University of South Florida, Tampa, FL. After college I started my first job earning $9.00 per hour. I recall thinking that this was not what I envision my life to be like after completing four years of college with minimal student loans. While in college I joined the ROTC program. Enlisted in Army Reserve after college and used the GI Bill to pay off my student loan debt. This was my first life experience- a light bulb opportunity to use systems already in place to my advantage.

I worked my way up the corporate ladder after expecting a position as a Florida state employee. During my tenure, I was presented with my first entrepreneurial opportunity in which I negotiated terms with seller. In October 1989, my first business partner and I were off and running as new childcare center owners. I worked the early shift with my state job so I could close the daycare in the evenings. That was working smoothly at first, until a bump in the road. My partner was nervous. She questioned putting money in the business versus earning a large salary. We both quickly learned that most small businesses fail within the first two years of operating. However, I refused to be included in a negative statistical number, especially after having had refinanced my first home to secure half the funds to purchase my first business. Glossing over several details, I bought my business partner out of her half of the childcare center ownership and hired additional staff. This was my first of several experiences with dismantling something to build back better.

Shortly after acquiring 100% of ownership of the childcare center, I received a call from a state investigator. I was being investigated for breach of a state policy. Not knowing any details, I was called to meet with an investigator. Of course, I sat in my car and prayed before I entered the building. The investigator asked if I knew why I was summoned. I said "No". As she read the allegations against me, I was stunned to learn that my supervisor with had been investigating the small business I operated outside my full-time job. Once I explained to the investigator that I never accepted funds or that the parent on complaint never signed a grievance with my business, the case was closed as null and void. In business, setbacks can change everything. Thankfully, that setback was a setup for a comeback. James 5:16 says, "The effectual fervent prayer of a righteous man availeth much."

> *Life is like a road, It has bumps, cracks, and obstacles*
> *But in the end, it gets you somewhere.*

Do not allow fear to decide your fate

After that investigation I was feeling some kind-a-way. After all, I thought I was an exemplary employee since I had great annual evaluations and reviews. However, the work environment turned sour quickly. My reviews were not so appealing, and it was clear that a few of the higher-ups were not happy with the outcome of the investigation. After much consideration, I resigned from my position with the state. During my exit interview, my supervisor wished me good luck. I was so happy to reply, "I don't need luck when I have God on my side". My true entrepreneurial journey had just begun.

I earned a real estate license in February 2000. My passion as a realtor is to educate others on how I used my first home to purchase my first business. Home ownership is a powerful tool if used correctly. This was another lightbulb opportunity. OPM, or Other People Money, is the most powerful tool I have learned to enhance my entrepreneurship journey.

In June 2005, I was reading a local weekly Flyer when I saw, "Cleaning business for sell". I called the number to inquire about business and asked if I could stop by to speak about the details. It was late in the evening, but I assured the woman on the other end of the call that I would not take up much of her time. She agreed to meet with me, and not only did she agree to sell me her business, but she also took the ad down while we talked for nearly two hours. When I asked if she needed a deposit before I left, she gave me an emphatic "No". Our spirits connected and the meeting ended with another business opportunity.

Do you have a strong desire to be your own boss?

The following Monday after meeting with the cleaning business owner, we meet at the franchisor corporate office. Once I paid franchise and transfer fees, I was the owner of a successful cleaning business. My career as a commercial janitorial company had begun and I inquired about additional accounts to expand the business. Honestly, I did not know anything about cleaning office spaces, but I did maintain a clean house so I thought it could not be that difficult to learn. I hopped into the business "all in." I quickly learned to clean nasty toilets and spent late nights dumping trash in dumpsters in dark spaces. Over the years, the business has grown with the helping hands of my dedicated team.

> *"You will always pass failure on your way to success."*
>
> **Mickey Rooney, American actor**

Financially, the real estate business has changed my life. I have purchased multiple properties as rental income. I have partnered with general contractors and secured commercial loans (OPM) to build single family homes. To expand the business, I even purchased properties in surrounding counties as investment opportunities for profit. With this, I have made strides. However, what I have learned is that few things in life are guaranteed. After growing too big too fast—I filed a Chapter 10 Bankruptcy. I did not realize it at the time, but I had to pay capital gain taxes to the IRS for profits earned when I sold my first rental property. I liquidated all my properties, including the vacant lots. This was a huge setback.

Giving up my first home was hard and emotional because that was the asset used to purchase my first business opportunity. During the consultation with the bankruptcy attorney, we reviewed accounts and properties I had acquired to that point. As I scanned the spreadsheets, I asked about the recurring number of 1.3K. The attorney replied, "That's your real estate net worth." I had earned my first million dollars in debit and did not even know it. During those five years of bankruptcy, I learned how to save and use my money more efficiently and effectively. Since that time, I have rebuilt my credit profile and only purchase items that are going to make my money grow.

After the bankruptcy discharge in 2015, I have managed to rebuild my real estate career—which is my first entrepreneurial passion. My cleaning business has tripled in revenue and staff. I am humbled by the commitment of my team. As a small appreciation for such a big commitment, I reward them with above average pay rates and build relationships that have been long lasting. I truly believe that my endeavors are a conduit for revenues that promotes opportunities for everyone to eat at the table. It has been a journey. I have learned that entrepreneurial is an adjective, characterized by taking financial risks in the hope of profit. That is enterprising.

> *"The true entrepreneur is a doer not a dreamer."*
>
> **Nolan Bushnell, American businessman**

Over the years I have been asked about mentorship opportunities. I am honored to have coached and mentored men and women on tools of the trades. I was blessed to leave a full-time career and have now sustained profitable incomes for myself and others for the past 17 years as a business owner. One of the first things that I say to the person asking for assistance is, "You have to put in the work". I remember reading somewhere that, "You get what you work for, not what you wish for". I believe this to be true, at least for me. I have seen friends and family start businesses that go under because they are not willing to get down in the trenches or on bended knees when necessary.

One of my biggest and raving fans is Sister Laura Julien, a church companion. She always reminds me that God blesses me because I genuinely love people and pour into the success of others. My success has been the grace and love of God. I can write an entire book about how God has placed me in the right places at the right times for success and blessings.

Power Moves

- Do not expect others to take greater risks for building your dreams than you are willing to take.

- Position yourself as the solution to someone else's problem.

- Beware of distractions—and opportunities too.

CHAPTER 17

Binika Henderson

Binika is available for conferences, workshops, panel discussions & seminars. She is a real estate mogul, having sold over 229 homes, flipped over 100 homes, and sold over 25 million in production. She specializes in property flipping, real estate investing, working with first time and repeat buyers, property, and Airbnb management. She provides the highest quality of personal service to meet the real estate needs of her clients. From residential marketing to investments, she can focus client's goals and achieve the results they desire. In addition, she is an educator, trainer, author, and speaker. She got her start in sales after graduating college but wanted to take command over my schedule and generate more income. In 2007, she got her real estate license and started selling properties for a large real estate company. Within a few months she closed her first sale and her excitement and entrepreneurial instincts drove her to launch her own real estate business, however, her dreams were put on pause when the market crashed. She found herself in a great deal of debt.

Binika continued to push forward, and over time, she recovered. She pushed aggressively to close deals and saved enough to purchase her first rental property. With the profit from her rental property and her sales skyrocketing, she started to think about what it would be like to own and operate her own real estate company. In 2013 and only 32 years-old, she founded Heritage Real Estate, a full-service real estate and property management company. The firm works with clients to generate 10x's a return on their investment in 60 days or less—leveraging other people's money.

Binika has been featured on several media outlets including the cover of Top Agent Magazine, Accion Chicago Annual Report and more. She is on a mission to educate the masses and share her strategies for success in a big way. Her new book, *Flipping Gary* will help aspiring and seasoned real estate professionals earn massive returns on their money using other people's money!

Always one to give back, Binika launched Binika Cares™, which gives back by assisting youth get internships and job opportunities through Work One and Goodwill. Additionally, her Heritage Helps™ program donates coats and blankets to local charities.

Binika earned a bachelor's degree in Industrial Psychology with Honors Distinction from Purdue University West Lafayette, Indiana. She is certified in the State of Indiana as a Certified Minority Business Owner, a Licensed Realtor® and Property Manager in the State of Indiana and Illinois, has CRS/RRC Residential Real Estate Council Designation, E-Pro Certification & Serves as a member on her local MLS Board of Directors for Greater Northwest Indiana Association of Realtors® & received a prestigious award in Northwest Indiana as Top 20 Under 40 in Business. She currently resides & operates her business Heritage Real Estate Services Inc. in Merrillville, IN.

The Power of **Bold**

The Power of a Bold Legacy

Real Estate Wealth

Binika Henderson
Real Estate Mogul

> *Hold fast to dreams For if dreams die Life is a broken-winged bird That cannot fly.*
>
> **Langston Hughes, American poet, playwright**

Bold is a great attribute to have in life as well as for your financial future goals. Real estate is a great tool to build an empire of generational wealth, building and leaving a long-term legacy for generations to come.

Make your life vision a priority. To live out the vision you have developed, you must keep your vision at the top of your priorities. *When making decisions in the future, consider options that will support your life vision.*

Developing your life vision will take time, reflection, and work, but the rewards will be great. *Your life will be filled with passion and optimism once you develop your vision.* Why wait? Start creating your vision today!

Did you know that 90% of millionaires have built their wealth by investing in real estate? I personally have found a great passion by educating myself by investing in different avenues of real estate. Real estate is a great addition to any portfolio for several reasons. Purchasing real estate gives you access to a stable source of income, provides you with assets that are highly valuable, and protects you against inflation. There is wealth in diversity

However, there are a few drawbacks when it comes to investing in real estate, including the fact that properties are not as liquid as other forms of investments. Meaning, once you invest, it is not an immediate return of investment. The return can be a longer time frame; however, the yield can be substantial. The market can fluctuate, and the initial investment is much higher than with other financial products. There are ways to get around this last drawback. **There are several strategies you can use to purchase real estate without a large down payment.** It is important to gain a solid understanding of these different strategies and to persevere.

> *"The best investment on earth is earth."*
>
> **- Louis Glickman, Real estate investor and philanthropist**

To be a savvy investor and stay ahead of the learning curve. A real estate investor needs to properly prepare him or herself as an investor and or landlord by learning all the laws—city, county, state, and federal—that govern being a landlord where your property is located.

According to Bigger Pockets: Landlord Station names Texas, Indiana, and Colorado as its top three landlord friendly states. Arizona and Florida are also on the list. Please note this system can be applied in any market, however this particularly worked for me in the Northwest Indiana market, more so in Gary, Indiana.

Preparation: Things to know before getting started when investing in real estate

Just like with any other type of investment, it is crucial to educate yourself before getting started. Investing in real estate without understanding what you are doing or being able to recognize good deals can be very costly. Before investing money in real estate, invest some time in researching the topic and educating yourself on creative financing.

1. **Creative financing works best if you can find great deals, since the potential for profit is greater.** Remember that paying full price on a property will result in higher mortgage payments, even if you do not have to make a down payment.

   - As a rule of thumb, always look for the best profit margin, put as little cash down as possible, and negotiate with the seller.

2. **Be conservative when using creative financing.** Several things could happen to reduce your profit margin. You might have to pay several thousands of dollars to have tenants evicted. You might encounter costly repairs or see taxes and interest rates go up.

   - Always plan for the worst scenario so, if it should happen, you can avoid losing money on a deal.

3. **Be ready to make sacrifices.** It is possible to buy real estate with little or no money down, but this does not mean you can get into real estate without working hard.

   - You will be successful if you are highly motivated, ready to learn about real estate, and willing to put time and effort into looking for deals and negotiating.

4. Put some money aside. You can get started with little or no money down, but you will still have expenses to cover in the long-term. You might have to pay for repairs or make up for a loss of income if a tenant is not paying their rent.

- Save up some money, ask for a raise, or look for a second job so you can build a comfortable cushion that will protect your investment from unforeseen expenses.

5. Learn as much as you can about real estate. There are plenty of resources available to you, including books, classes, seminars, and online material. Take some time to learn about the market, how to recognize good deals, how to negotiate, and gain a better understanding of different creative financing strategies.

6. Should you invest in a property that is ready to move into, or look for one in need of repairs? This is an important question to ask yourself before you get started.

- A move-in-ready property is usually more expensive, but you will be able to start renting it right away.

- A property in need of repairs should be more affordable, but you will have to invest time and money in repairs before you can even start renting it out.

> *"You ought to be able to explain why you're taking the job you're taking, why you are making the investment you are making, or whatever it may be. And if it cannot stand applying pencil to paper, you'd better think it through some more. And if you cannot write an intelligent answer to those questions, don't do it."*
>
> **- Warren Buffett, CEO Berkshire Hathaway**

COVID-19 investing: When financial times are difficult

The final pages of this chapter were developed during the very troubling times in 2020 during the financial crisis of COVID-19.

When times are tough and money is tight, one of the first things you may neglect is investing. That is also true when there is volatility in the stock market or when real estate prices seem to be dropping. People get frightened, and they do not want to take the risk. You do not have to stop investing, though. *You just must be more cautious.*

Investing is a great way to build up a nest egg for the future. *If you take the time to put money into investments that are safe, you will not have to be as concerned about losing your cash.*

When the economic climate improves, the stock market and real estate market can help you make money very quickly, but that is not the case when there are very few hot stocks and no one's buying houses!

Banks can help you in a down market

You may not think of savings accounts as much of an investment because of their low interest rates. When you want to protect your money, though, it is better to put it into something that offers a lower return and virtually no risk, as opposed to something that's high risk. *A savings account will not make you rich, but you will earn a steady return and will not need to worry.*

While you are at the bank, ask about CDs and IRAs. These are both ways to save for retirement and get a modest return while keeping your money protected. A CD, or Certificate of Deposit, typically pays a higher interest rate than a savings account. You must leave the money alone for a while, but many CDs are short-term investments.

Other ways to invest

Some people also make private loans to others. These can be risky, but if you know and trust the person, you are loaning money to, you can make a loan with the cash you have and get payments with interest. It is not quite the same as investing in stocks or real estate, but you are investing in the future of someone who needs your help—and making money in the process.

Others invest their money by playing games of chance. However, *it is never safe to gamble more than you can afford to lose.* In a down economy, the amount you can afford to lose will likely be at or near zero. Only when you have money to play with should you consider trying to make money by gambling, instead of saving.

Giving up is not the answer

The most important thing to remember is that the economy *will* improve. While you might not be making the return on your investment that you had hoped for, that can (and most likely will) change in the future.

Keep thinking positive and looking into new investment options. Talk to your banker or financial adviser about saving money and earning a good return on it.

Listen to the suggestions you are given and choose the best ones for you. Remember, investing is not just about making a quick buck. *It is about a long-term strategy.* You may need it one day. If not, you can use it to travel, help family members who need it, or donate to a charity that matters to you.

If you invest carefully and do not lock yourself into something long-term that might not be right for you, you will come out ahead in the end. Be prepared to lose a bit from time to time. That happens to even the best investors. *By proceeding with caution and cutting losses when necessary, you should be able to continue to invest even in hard financial times.*

House flipping rules you must know

House flipping has become a trendy way to earn extra money, but you must be careful. For your best results, it is critical to be aware of these important tips.

House flipping can add an extra income stream for your family. However, it is important to approach this business carefully and be aware of the disadvantages. Next, we will progress into the 7 Steps to Making Money Fast through Quick Flips and Wealth Building.

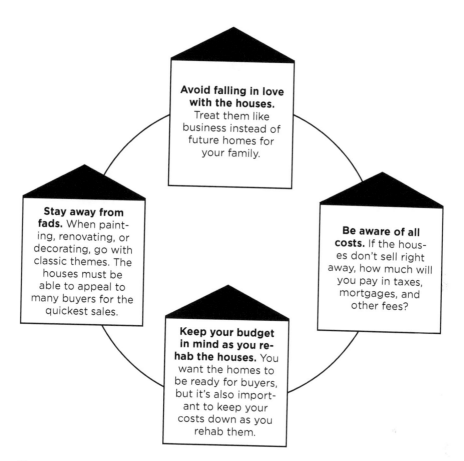

Avoid falling in love with the houses. Treat them like business instead of future homes for your family.

Stay away from fads. When painting, renovating, or decorating, go with classic themes. The houses must be able to appeal to many buyers for the quickest sales.

Be aware of all costs. If the houses don't sell right away, how much will you pay in taxes, mortgages, and other fees?

Keep your budget in mind as you rehab the houses. You want the homes to be ready for buyers, but it's also important to keep your costs down as you rehab them.

Step 1: Property Financing

First step, you want to consider how you will be financing your investment and your budget for your property and renovations.

- Need a lender? Are you using your own cash?

- What is your budget for the earnest money, property and what is your budget for any renovations?

- What is your preferred area and home criteria? How many rooms, how many square feet?

- Do you have funding sources or help if the project stalls or goes over budget?

- Things to note. ALWAYS have a backup plan for the unforeseen for the project. As much as you plan and organize, as you get into the project there is the unforeseen, just set aside additional funding for the just in case.

- Additional sources can be you and a partner, a credit card or savings set aside for this project. Just do not start this process if this money is to be used for your personal bills and will set you behind.

1. **Private money is a very popular form of creative financing.** Private money refers to money you get from another investor, such as a friend or family member. *This strategy is interesting if you can find an affordable home and can negotiate the right terms with the investor you borrow from.* Ensure you get everything written in a detailed contract.

2. **Hard money lenders can provide you with the money you need to invest in real estate if you are willing to pay high fees.** The downside of hard money loans is that you do not have much time to pay the loan back. *However, it is possible to make a profit by having your property re-appraised:*

   - Borrow enough to purchase a home in need of repairs. Some hard money lenders will let you borrow 100% of the home value and enough to cover repairs on top of that.

   - Pay for repairs, look for ways to make the property more valuable, and have it appraised.

- Look for a refinancing option now that the property is worth more.

- Use your refinancing option to pay back what you borrowed from a hard money lender.

- Plan a good exit strategy in case the appraisal is not as high as you hoped.

1. **Using a line of credit is a good way to find creative financing for real estate deals.** The best way to obtain a good line of credit is to use your home for credit. Once you are approved for a line of credit, you will be able to pull money at any time without explaining what you will be using it for.

2. **Credit cards are ideal if you want to buy and flip a house in a short timeframe.** Use credit cards to get cash advances to cover a down payment or repairs. *Credit cards usually have high interest rates, but you can reduce costs by looking for another credit card that allows for balance transfer.*

- This strategy will allow you to avoid paying interest for at least the first year. Look for cards with a good reward program to get the most out of this creative financing strategy.

"People are living longer than ever before, a phenomenon undoubtedly made necessary by the 30-year mortgage."

- Doug Larson, American journalist

Using equity

You can use your current portfolio or assets for creative financing. This means you are taking the risk of losing your current portfolio or assets, but it can be worth it to take this risk if you come across a good deal.

There are different ways to use equity for creative financing:

1. **With proceeds from a refinance.** This strategy works if you have equity in your home and are willing to refinance it. You can then use the money to purchase an investment property.

   - This strategy works best if you were able to purchase your home below the market value and if the market values are currently high and the interest rates low.

2. **By borrowing against your family's equity.** Find a family member who is willing to help you by letting you refinance their home. Make sure you fill out a mortgage repayment plan or the IRS will look at the transaction as a gift.

3. **By investing through a self-directed IRA.** If you have one of these retirement accounts, you can invest in property with it. Use the money you put away in your IRA to make a down payment and have the rent or sale money deposited in your IRA later. You can also do this with a self-directed 401K.

4. **By taking a loan against your 401K.** The downside is that the money you borrow against your 401K will not be earning interests until you pay it back. *If you lose your job, you will have to put the money back in the 401K within a short timeframe or face penalties.*

5. By taking a security-backed loan. If you have a portfolio of stocks and other financial products, you can borrow up to 80% of its value. The interest rate should not exceed 5%. The downside is that you cannot sell your portfolio until the loan is paid off, but you will get your original portfolio back once you are done making payments.

> "Real estate investing, even on a very small scale, remains a tried-and-true means of building an individual's cash flow and wealth."
>
> **Robert Kiyosaki, American finance author, investor**

Step 2: Property Search/Scouting for Properties

Let us find your perfect investment home! You will be sent emails daily with your matched criteria. When you find the ones that you are ready to see, schedule with us and our licensed Realtor will be ready to take you on a showing. Since this program is designed with specific criteria in mind, we will customize your search to maximize your profit and to minimize the time in the process. If you are not local this program can still work for you!

Investing in out-of-state real estate

Despite the subject titled book- Flipping Gary, we encourage you to consider flipping in Gary with our team even if you are out of state or out of the country. Gary, IN offers higher yields on investments and you can join the large group of investors and increase your overall net worth. Currently Binika assists customers all throughout the USA and internationally at a great success rate.

Let us be realistic, buying real estate rarely goes smoothly and buying property out-of-state has even more potential challenges. However, it is entirely manageable if the potential trouble areas are planned for and addressed. Many people own property out-of-state, and you can too.

Reasons for buying out-of-state real estate

There are several reasons why you might consider owning a property in another state. Maybe local real estate prices are simply too high to qualify for a loan on a second home or investment property. Perhaps another area of the country is experiencing a real estate boom. Maybe you have a desire to own a vacation home.

Potential challenges

1. **Lack of knowledge about the area and the local economic situation.** Everyone knows what areas of their hometown are doing well and which areas are struggling. Successful real estate investors usually know more about the area of town in which they invest than the realtors do.

You will not have this type of day-to-day knowledge and will have to rely on others for their advice and opinions. Ensure you are getting your advice from a worthy source.

2. **You do not know the laws, regulations, property taxes, and other details.** Real estate laws and practices vary from state to state and even from city to city. Even more challenging, what is written in the codes and ordinances might not be the actual practice. You are going to have to find a way to gain this knowledge.

3. **Everything is going to cost more.** For a non-occupant owner, interest rates, down payment, and insurance are all higher. The banks simply don't have as much faith in a property owner that doesn't live in the property.

4. **You need an out-of-state team.** You are likely to need a property manager, handyman, real estate agent, project manager and more. Your team will have a huge impact on the level of success you experience. Build your team *before* you buy anything. Which is what your Real Estate Coach Binika Henderson has done for you right here in GARY INDIANA!

Things you must do

1. If you decide to keep your investment property... **Hire an excellent property manager.** If you are going to rent out your property, keep in mind that an investment rental property is only as good as its management. It is important to find someone that you can trust even when you are not there. I may be a little bias here but... Heritage Real Estate Services Inc. Property Management division is at the

heart of the organization. We take property management seriously and put the needs of our landlords first. We have full time staff that covers all areas of Property Management to ensure your property is properly maintained.

Property management includes making decisions about repairs, filling vacancies, evictions, and handling any other problems that may arise unexpectedly or even in the middle of the night.

2. **See the property before you buy it.** While very experienced investors frequently do not, it is still a good idea to see the property before you buy it. Until you have a team you can trust, you do not really know what you are getting until you see it yourself.

3. **Visit the area.** If possible, get out to the area and arm yourself with a local map. Spend a couple of days driving around, getting the lay of the land, and asking a lot of questions. Meet a couple of real estate agents and landowners. Set these appointments up prior to arrival to save time.

4. **Join the local real estate investors club.** REIA is a common local investment club based throughout each state. They are a great way to meet with likeminded people & even meet new friends. Even if you are buying a vacation home, these are the people that know the area, trends, and relevant people. One good friend in the local club is invaluable. Join and make a friend. One of the local REIA groups located near Gary, IN that I am personally a part of is NICIA Northwest Indiana Creative Investors Association. Check them out at www.nicia.org.

Owning property out-of-state can be a wonderful investment from either a financial or enjoyment standpoint.

As with anything else, if you understand the potential challenges beforehand and prepare for them, your likelihood of success is much greater. Be sure to get your team in place (such as Heritage Real Estate Services) do your due diligence, know as much about the area as you possibly can & get going. Good luck! Be sure to check out heritagerealestateservices.com for all real estate investing needs!

Step 3: Make an Offer!

After you have seen all your preferred properties, you have found the one and are ready to make an offer! Once your offer is accepted, be ready to submit your earnest money, usually within 48-72 hours. Be sure it is in Certified Funds unless instructed differently.

Step 4: Property Inspection

Now it is time to have your home inspected. This is usually done and scheduled by you so that you can be present. You can choose to not have an inspection if you are okay with the aesthetic condition of the property because it will be inspected again through The Program once accepted. Getting an inspection prior solely allows you to know beforehand what the condition of the home is before you purchase the home. These usual cost you $300- $400.

Step 5: Closing Day. Congrats... Calculate Your Estimated Profit Before Closing

Now it's time for closing day. You now have the keys to your new investment property! Therefore, you will need homeowner's insurance. It is your responsibility to have this done effective the day of closing.

Another important aspect to a successful real estate investment is to calculate how much money you will make through this journey. Look at the formula below, you can use this tool to successfully formulate your ROI.

How to calculate ROI for real estate investments

ROI or *Return on Investment* is a term used to describe how much you profit from an investment. *It is the percentage of money made on an investment after all the costs associated with that investment are subtracted.* So, if you invested $10 and earned $1, your ROI would be 10%, assuming you get your original $10 back.

The basic equation is:

$$\frac{(\text{Gain} - \text{Investment Cost}) \times 100\%}{\text{Your Cost}}$$

Let's look at the two basic methods of applying this equation to real estate investments:

1. The Out-of-Pocket Method

Suppose you purchased a house for $100,000. The needed re-hab was $60,000 and the eventual selling price was $200,000. Let's also assume that the investor only had to come up with a $10,000 down payment and the rehab costs.

The ROI would be:

$$\frac{(\$200,000 - \$160,000) \times 100\% = {\sim}57\%}{\$70,000}$$

2. The Cost Method

Let us use the same imaginary situation, but the investor paid for everything with his own money.

The equity in the property is
$40,000 (200,000 − 100,000 − 60,000= $40,000).

The ROI would be $40,000 / $160,000 = 25%

(A 40k profit on 160k spent).

The first method allows for the use of leverage, so it might seem better to borrow as much as you can. But consider that that ac-tual amount of money you would make would be greater in #2, since there would not be any costs associated with the loan. So, your rate of return might be lower, but the number of dollars in your pocket would be greater.

Which method you choose is up to you. The point is to stick to one method when comparing different prospective invest-ments. *ROI can be an excellent tool to determine which deal is better than another.*

Other considerations

Do not be concerned with equity in your calculations; *it is better to be concerned with the amount of money you are left with at the end.* You need to consider all your expenses, such as:

- Property taxes that you must pay

- Insurance while you are holding the property.

- Utilities

- Interest on any loans

- Closing costs, both to buy and to sell the property

- Real estate commissions when you sell

- Mowing the grass until the property sells

- Appraisal and inspection costs

  - Costs for repairs—both materials and labor

The real estate shows you see on TV rarely address all these costs. All they talk about is the purchase price, cost of repairs, and the selling price. As you can see, repair costs are only one of many costs that you may be responsible for. Those shows have nothing to do with reality. *Be sure you are subtracting all your expected costs when you do your calculations.*

Also consider time. Is a 40% return in 12 months better than a 20% return in 12 weeks? In most cases, no, it is not. Just be sure to consider the time when you're making comparisons.

Also consider cash flow. In the case of an apartment building, your 'gain' would be the rents that you collect over the course of a year. But be sure to include a vacancy rate in your calculations. There are also greater costs associated with owning rental properties: repairs in the middle of the night, painting between tenants, advertising, carpeting, landscaping, and more.

Getting an accurate ROI estimate really is not possible in real estate. You never truly know your future selling price or how long it will take. Repair estimates can be off as well. That is why *it is important to estimate high on your costs and low on the income.* Be conservative and you will always be pleasantly surprised.

Step 6: Getting the Home Ready to Go! Let's Get Ready to Sell and/or Rent

If your property needs a little TLC, project managing, lawn/yard maintenance or cleaning, we can assist! We also will list and show your property. Our rates are 10% or $100 minimum of the rent and the first month's rent for the placement fee. The rent must be a minimum of $675/month. Fortunately, our properties usually rent fast. While it is on the market for leasing you can expect to get an offer from an investor through THE PROGRAM.

Step 7: Road to Success...What's Next?

Exit Strategy, Sale, Rent, Cash out Refi, sell via the Program, Covid-19 New Challenges, Tax Consequences, Analyzing the deal, your next deal, continuing with Heritage, Additional coaching, Flipping Plan Strategy, O- Zones, Self-Directed IRA's. Advanced Training.

Power Moves

- Focus on generational wealth—both financially and in the values you demonstrate.

- Invest in you and in the future of those you love.

- Calculate the ROI in every area of your life.

APPENDIX

Make Your Power Moves

Interactive Exercises

FREEDOM

lies in being

BOLD.

Robert Frost, American poet

Create a bold image of yourself. What is that bold image doing differently than what you are currently doing?

Make a plan to act boldly in an area where you have been avoiding conflict or confrontation.

You are much bolder than you think. Make a note of your most recent memory of going outside your comfort zone. What pushed you outside your usual boundary?

You can not change what you do not acknowledge. When you think about a risk you have contemplating, what scary thoughts come up for you?

Thought:

_____

_____

_____

Thought:

_____

_____

_____

Thought:

_____

_____

_____

Know thyself. Make a list of your strengths.

1. _____

2. _____

3. _____

4. _____

5. _____

6. _____

7. _____

8. _____

9. _____

10. _____

What are your greatest assets (resources you own or control like skills, personality, etc.)? Ask those around you for input on this one. What shows up that you did not identify as a strength?

1. _____

2. _____

3. _____

4. _____

5. _____

6. _____

7. _____

8. _____

9. _____

10. _____

The Power of **Bold**

Keep your eyes on the prize. What decision(s) can you make in the next 6 months that have the potential to render you the greatest ROC (return on choice)?

_____

_____

_____

_____

_____

_____

_____

_____

_____

Intention is important. How do you intend to show up in the world?

_____

_____

_____

_____

_____

_____

_____

_____

_____

Practice confidence.

- ☐ Be mindful of your posture. Sit and stand tall.
- ☐ Project your voice.
- ☐ Maintain appropriate eye contact.
- ☐ Head up, shoulders back, and swing those arms with control.
- ☐ Pick up your pace to walk with a swaggin' stride.
- ☐ Smile, smile, smile.

Sell yourself. Self-talk creates pathways in the brain when re-peated. Write four affirmations and repeat a different one each week over the next 20 days.

1. _____

_____

2. _____

_____

3. _____

_____

4. _____

_____

I AM breathed His breath into your nostrils and there was life (Genesis 2:7). Use colorful, creative, and bold words to describe who you are (your personality). Examples include bubbly, yummy, vivacious, exquisite, dashing, daring, etc.

I am _____

I am _____

I am _____

I am _____

I am _____

I am _____

I am _____

Bold acts require you do to something different. This week, change your routine from your norm (maybe your morning routine, drive to or from work, the way you approach something at work, etc.). On a scale of 0 to 10, 0 = not difficult at all and 10 = very difficult, how difficult was this change in your routine?

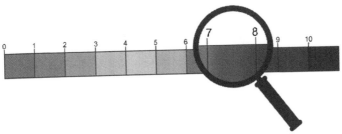

Act important—because you are. When you look important, it is easier to feel important. This week, choose a day to dress like you Live Big! Plan your attire here.

_____

_____

_____

_____

_____

According to Jim Rohn, motivational speaker, "You are the average of the five people you spend the most time with." List the five people you spend the most time with and identify how they influence you.

1. _____ influence is..._____

2. _____ influence is..._____

3. _____ influence is..._____

4. _____ influence is..._____

5. _____ influence is..._____

What is the last thing you did to celebrate an accomplish (small or big)? Celebrations fuel greater accomplishments. Take time to celebrate small wins and maximize the energy to become even bolder. Plan your celebration here.

I am celebrating _____

This celebration is special because: _____

_____

_____

_____

Date: _____Time: _____

Place: _____

Invitees:

_____

_____

_____

_____

_____

Vince Lombardi, former NFL coach, would say, *"It's not the size of the dog in the fight, but the size of the fight in the dog"!* Repeat Lombardi's mantra several times out loud. Make a note of what comes to mind for you as you think about obstacles you may be facing.

AUTHOR DIRECTORY

Tammy L. Allen
TLA Enterprise of Tampa Bay LLC
www.tlaenterprise.com

Terri L. Bailey, Colonel
United States Airforce

Kay Bodude, RN, BSN
Best Care Behavioral Homes, Co-owner
www.kaybodude.com

Brittany Browne, RN, BSN

Educator, Energizer, Healer
info@brittanybrowne.com
IG: @iambrittanybrowne
Facebook: Brittany Browne

Alicia Delgado-Gavin, PsyD

Psychologist, Licensed Marriage & Family Therapist, Speaker
dr.delgado@tearsbehindthesmile.com
IG: @draliciadelgadogavin
Phone: 631-639-8227
www.aliciadelgadogavin.com

India Gary-Martin

Leadership for Execs, CEO & Founder
www.leadershipforexecs.com

Binika Henderson
Real Estate Mogul
www.binikahenderson.com

Sharon T. Hoskins, Esq.
MyMotivationNation.com

Eboni Isaacs
Salon 33 Hair Restoration Salon/Clinic, Owner

Jennifer Jackson
Fitness Coach
Fit4fifties@gmail.com
www.fitforfifties.com

Wendy Labat, DBA
The Financial Healer
www.thefinancialcures.com

Kendale M. McDaniel
www.FullyArmedFitness.com

Theresa Noach
Singer, Songwriter, Speaker
www.daughterofnaomi.com

Malik Parker
Certified Peer Specialist

Christina Rampersad
Success Beyond the Brink, Founder
www.successbeyondthebrink.com

Eileen Cooper Reed, Esq.
The Intersections Group, Founder
www.philanthropyohio.org

Yvette Vega
Endorphins Mind Body System, Creator

Compiled by

Larthenia Howard, EdD
The Stimuknowlogy Institute LLC
www.lartheniahoward.com
www.anchorofhopetherapy.com
www.FromABookToABusiness.com

Larthenia Howard, EdD

Dr. Larthenia Howard is a two-time award-winning author and creator of the How to Write a Book in 31 Days System©—a step-by-step process that shows aspiring authors how to create value-add content that attracts visibility and expands influence. In her more recently developed course, From a Book to a Business©, she teaches authors how to create multiple streams of income from a book, and grow a business beyond the pages.

Larthenia has been featured on TBN Network, The Lee Pitts Show, National Association of Secondary School Principals periodical, Professional Women Network platform, and national and local syndicated broadcasts. She is host of the Dr. Empowerment Blog Talk Radio Show and certified as a Neuro-Linguistic Programming (NLP) Master Practitioner and Emotional Intelligence Facilitator.

Prior to becoming an author and entrepreneur, Dr. Howard served as an English teacher, professor, and as a member of the National No Child Left Behind Task Force in Washington, D.C., where she was instrumental in legislative recommendations for education reform.

Five Fun Facts About Larthenia:

- A skateboarder, or as she says, "A lover of Land Yachts"
- Enjoys exploration in caves around the world
- Favorite pastime is a leisure walk in a botanical garden
- Collects rocks from places she visits
- Goes bananas for a Woodwick candle

222   The Power of **Bold**